David Sedaris is the author of the books *Barrel Fever,* *Santaland Diaries, Holidays on Ice, Dress Your Family in Corduroy and Denim, When You Are Engulfed in Flames, Squirrel Seeks, Chipmunk, Let's Explore Diabetes with Owls* and *Theft by Finding,* and is a regular contributor to *This American Life* and BBC Radio 4.

Praise for ME TALK PRETTY ONE DAY

'A humorist par excellence, he can make Woody Allen appear ham-tongued, Oscar Wilde a drag . . . Sedaris is seriously funny . . . [his] autobiographical Chinese whispers continue to take telling tales to sublime heights' *Observer*

'[Sedaris] is excellent company and relentlessly good-natured. His sophistication is spiked with self-doubt, and his insouciance has a tremor of the unhinged' *Independent*

'A funny and intelligent strip-search of the human psyche' *Arena*

'Crammed full of deadpan vitriol, New Yorker David Sedaris rattles off this latest batch of bordering-on-fiction tales of his dysfunctional life . . . Sedaris writes like the Grinch on crystal meth and the punchline is usually himself . . . Sedaris is the master of the shaggy dog story' *Face*

KT-237-477

ALSO BY DAVID SEDARIS

Barrel Fever
Naked
Santaland Diaries
Dress Your Family in Corduroy and Denim
When You Are Engulfed in Flames
Squirrel Seeks Chipmunk
Let's Explore Diabetes with Owls
Theft by Finding
Calypso

(also available as audiobooks)

Me Talk Pretty

One Day

David Sedaris

ABACUS

First published in the United States of America by
Little, Brown and Company US in 2000
First published in Great Britain by Abacus in 2001
This edition published in 2002

37 39 40 38 36

Copyright © David Sedaris 2000

The moral right of the author has been asserted.

All rights reserved.
No part of this publication may be reproduced, stored in a
retrieval system, or transmitted, in any form or by any means, without
the prior permission in writing of the publisher, nor be otherwise circulated
in any form of binding or cover other than that in which it is published
and without a similar condition including this condition being
imposed on the subsequent purchaser.

Acknowledgement is made to the following, in which various
forms of this book's pieces first appeared.

New Yorker: "Genetic Engineering" • *Esquire:* "You Can't Kill the Rooster," "The Youth in
Asia," "A Shiner Like a Diamond," "Big Boy," "Me Talk Pretty One Day," "Jesus Shaves,"
"I'll Eat What He's Wearing," "Smart Guy" • "This American Life": "Giant Dreams,
Midget Abilities," "Twelve Moments in the Life of the Artist," • BBC Radio 4: "The Great
Leap Forward," "Today's Special," "City of Angels," "The Tapeworm Is In"

A CIP catalogue record for this book is available from the British Library.

ISBN 978-0-349-11391-3

Typeset by M Rules
Printed and bound in Great Britain by Clays Ltd, Elcograf S.p.A.

Papers used by Abacus are from well-managed forests
and other responsible sources.

Abacus
An imprint of
Little, Brown Book Group
Carmelite House
50 Victoria Embankment
London EC4Y 0DZ

An Hachette UK Company
www.hachette.co.uk

www.littlebrown.co.uk

For my father, Lou

Contents

Deux

Me Talk Pretty One Day

One

Go Carolina

ANYONE WHO WATCHES EVEN THE SLIGHTEST amount of TV is familiar with the scene: An agent knocks on the door of some seemingly ordinary home or office. The door opens, and the person holding the knob is asked to identify himself. The agent then says, "I'm going to ask you to come with me."

They're always remarkably calm, these agents. If asked "Why do I need to go anywhere with you?" they'll straighten their shirt cuffs or idly brush stray hairs from the sleeves of their sport coats and say, "Oh, I think we both know why."

The suspect then chooses between doing things the hard way and doing things the easy way, and the scene ends with either gunfire or the gentlemanly application of handcuffs. Occasionally it's a case of mistaken identity, but most often the suspect knows exactly why he's being taken. It seems he's been expecting this to happen. The anticipation has ruled his life, and now, finally, the wait is over. You're sometimes led to believe that this person is actually relieved, but I've never bought it. Though it probably has its moments, the average day spent in hiding is bound to beat the average day spent in prison. When it comes time to decide who gets the bottom bunk, I think anyone would agree that there's a lot to be said for doing things the hard way.

The agent came for me during a geography lesson. She entered the room and nodded at my fifth-grade teacher, who stood frowning at a map of Europe. What would needle me later was the realization that this had all been prearranged. My capture had been scheduled to go down at exactly 2:30 on a Thursday afternoon. The agent would be wearing a dung-colored blazer over a red knit turtleneck, her heels sensibly low in case the suspect should attempt a quick getaway.

"David," the teacher said, "this is Miss Samson, and she'd like you to go with her now."

No one else had been called, so why me? I ran down a list of recent crimes, looking for a conviction that might stick. Setting fire to a reportedly flameproof Halloween costume, stealing a set of barbecue tongs from an unguarded patio, altering the word *hit* on a list of rules posted on the gymnasium door; never did it occur to me that I might be innocent.

"You might want to take your books with you," the teacher said. "And your jacket. You probably won't be back before the bell rings."

Though she seemed old at the time, the agent was most

likely fresh out of college. She walked beside me and asked what appeared to be an innocent and unrelated question: "So, which do you like better, State or Carolina?"

She was referring to the athletic rivalry between the Triangle area's two largest universities. Those who cared about such things tended to express their allegiance by wearing either Tar Heel powder blue, or Wolf Pack red, two colors that managed to look good on no one. The question of team preference was common in our part of North Carolina, and the answer supposedly spoke volumes about the kind of person you either were or hoped to become. I had no interest in football or basketball but had learned it was best to pretend otherwise. If a boy didn't care for barbecued chicken or potato chips, people would accept it as a matter of personal taste, saying, "Oh well, I guess it takes all kinds." You could turn up your nose at the president or Coke or even God, but there were names for boys who didn't like sports. When the subject came up, I found it best to ask which team my questioner preferred. Then I'd say, "Really? Me, too!"

Asked by the agent which team I supported, I took my cue from her red turtleneck and told her that I was for State. "Definitely State. State all the way."

It was an answer I would regret for years to come.

"State, did you say?" the agent asked.

"Yes, State. They're the greatest."

"I see." She led me through an unmarked door near the principal's office, into a small, windowless room furnished with two facing desks. It was the kind of room where you'd grill someone until they snapped, the kind frequently painted so as to cover the bloodstains. She gestured toward what was to become my regular seat, then continued her line of questioning.

"And what exactly are they, State and Carolina?"

"Colleges? Universities?"

She opened a file on her desk, saying, "Yes, you're right. Your answers are correct, but you're saying them incorrectly. You're telling me that they're college*th* and univer*thitieth*, when actually they're college*s* and universitie*s*. You're giving me a *th* sound instead of a nice clear *s*. Can you hear the distinction between the two different sound*s*?"

I nodded.

"May I please have an actual an*s*wer?"

"Uh-huh."

" 'Uh-huh' i*s* not a word."

"Okay."

"Okay what?"

"Okay," I said. "Sure, I can hear it."

"You can hear what, the distinction? The contra*s*t?"

"Yeah, that."

It was the first battle of my war against the letter *s*, and I was determined to dig my foxhole before the sun went down. According to Agent Samson, a "state certified speech therapist," my *s* was sibilate, meaning that I lisped. This was not news to me.

"Our goal i*s* to work together until eventually you can speak correctly," Agent Samson said. She made a great show of enunciating her own sparkling *s*'s, and the effect was profoundly irritating. "I'm trying to help you, but the longer you play these little games the longer this is going to take."

The woman spoke with a heavy western North Carolina accent, which I used to discredit her authority. Here was a person for whom the word *pen* had two syllables. Her people undoubtedly drank from clay jugs and hollered for Paw when the vittles were ready — so who was she to advise me on anything? Over the coming years I would find a crack in each of the therapists sent to train what Miss Samson now defined as my lazy tongue. "That's its problem," she said. "It's just plain lazy."

My sisters Amy and Gretchen were, at the time, undergoing therapy for their lazy eyes, while my older sister, Lisa, had been born with a lazy leg that had refused to grow at the same rate as its twin. She'd worn a corrective brace for the first two years of her life, and wherever she roamed she left a trail of scratch marks in the soft pine floor. I liked the idea that a part of one's body might be thought of as lazy — not thoughtless or hostile, just unwilling to extend itself for the betterment of the team. My father often accused my mother of having a lazy mind, while she in turn accused him of having a lazy index finger, unable to dial the phone when he knew damn well he was going to be late.

My therapy sessions were scheduled for every Thursday at 2:30, and with the exception of my mother, I discussed them with no one. The word *therapy* suggested a profound failure on my part. Mental patients had therapy. Normal people did not. I didn't see my sessions as the sort of thing that one would want to advertise, but as my teacher liked to say, "I guess it takes all kinds." Whereas my goal was to keep it a secret, hers was to inform the entire class. If I got up from my seat at 2:25, she'd say, "Sit back down, David. You've still got five minutes before your speech therapy session." If I remained seated until 2:27, she'd say, "David, don't forget you have a speech therapy session at two-thirty." On the days I was absent, I imagined she addressed the room, saying, "David's not here today but if he were, he'd have a speech therapy session at two-thirty."

My sessions varied from week to week. Sometimes I'd spend the half hour parroting whatever Agent Samson had to say. We'd occasionally pass the time examining charts on tongue position or reading childish s-laden texts recounting the adventures of seals or settlers named Sassy or Samuel. On the worst of days she'd haul out a tape recorder and show me just how much progress I was failing to make.

"My speech therapist's name is Miss Chrissy Samson." She'd hand me the microphone and lean back with her arms crossed. "Go ahead, say it. I want you to hear what you sound like."

She was in love with the sound of her own name and seemed to view my speech impediment as a personal assault. If I wanted to spend the rest of my life as David Thedarith, then so be it. She, however, was going to be called Miss Chrissy Samson. Had her name included no s's, she probably would have bypassed a career in therapy and devoted herself to yanking out healthy molars or performing unwanted clitoridectomies on the schoolgirls of Africa. Such was her personality.

"Oh, come on," my mother would say. "I'm sure she's not *that* bad. Give her a break. The girl's just trying to do her job."

I was a few minutes early one week and entered the office to find Agent Samson doing her job on Garth Barclay, a slight, kittenish boy I'd met back in the fourth grade. "You may wait outside in the hallway until it *is* your turn," she told me. A week or two later my session was interrupted by mincing Steve Bixler, who popped his head in the door and announced that his parents were taking him out of town for a long weekend, meaning that he would miss his regular Friday session. "Thorry about that," he said.

I started keeping watch over the speech therapy door, taking note of who came and went. Had I seen one popular student leaving the office, I could have believed my mother and viewed my lisp as the sort of thing that might happen to anyone. Unfortunately, I saw no popular students. Chuck Coggins, Sam Shelton, Louis Delucca: obviously, there was some connection between a sibilate *s* and a complete lack of interest in the State versus Carolina issue.

None of the therapy students were girls. They were all boys like me who kept movie star scrapbooks and made their own curtains. "You don't want to be doing that," the men in our families would say. "That's a girl thing." Baking scones and cupcakes for the school janitors, watching *Guiding Light* with our mothers, collecting rose petals for use in a fragrant potpourri: anything worth doing turned out to be a girl thing. In order to enjoy ourselves, we learned to be duplicitous. Our stacks of *Cosmopolitan* were topped with an unread issue of *Boy's Life* or *Sports Illustrated*, and our decoupage projects were concealed beneath the sporting equipment we never asked for but always received. When asked what we wanted to be when we grew up, we hid the truth and listed who we wanted to sleep with when we grew up. "A policeman or a fireman or one of those guys who works with high-tension wires." Symptoms were feigned, and our mothers wrote notes excusing our absences on the day of the intramural softball tournament. Brian had a stomach virus or Ted suffered from that twenty-four-hour bug that seemed to be going around.

"One of these days I'm going to have to hang a sign on that door," Agent Samson used to say. She was probably thinking along the lines of SPEECH THERAPY LAB, though a more appropriate marker would have read FUTURE HOMOSEXUALS OF AMERICA. We knocked ourselves out trying to fit in but were ultimately betrayed by our tongues. At the beginning of the school year, while we were congratulating ourselves on successfully passing for normal, Agent Samson was taking names as our assembled teachers raised their hands, saying, "I've got one in my homeroom," and "There are two in my fourth-period math class." Were they also able to spot the future drunks and depressives? Did they hope that by eliminating our lisps, they might set us on a different path, or were they trying to prepare us for future stage and choral careers?

Miss Samson instructed me, when forming an *s*, to position the tip of my tongue against the rear of my top teeth, right up against the gum line. The effect produced a sound not unlike that of a tire releasing air. It was awkward and strange-sounding, and elicited much more attention than the original lisp. I failed to see the hissy *s* as a solution to the problem and continued to talk normally, at least at home, where my lazy tongue fell upon equally lazy ears. At school, where every teacher was a potential spy, I tried to avoid an *s* sound whenever possible. "Yes," became "correct," or a military "affirmative." "Please," became "with your kind permission," and questions were pleaded rather than asked. After a few weeks of what she called "endless pestering" and what I called "repeated badgering," my mother bought me a pocket thesaurus, which provided me with *s*-free alternatives to just about everything. I consulted the book both at home in my room and at the daily learning academy other people called our school. Agent Samson was not amused when I began referring to her as an articulation coach, but the majority of my teachers were delighted. "What a nice vocabulary," they said. "My goodness, such big words!"

Plurals presented a considerable problem, but I worked around them as best I could; "rivers," for example, became either "a river or two" or "many a river." Possessives were a similar headache, and it was easier to say nothing than to announce that the left-hand and the right-hand glove of Janet had fallen to the floor. After all the compliments I had received on my improved vocabulary, it seemed prudent to lie low and keep my mouth shut. I didn't want anyone thinking I was trying to be a pet of the teacher.

When I first began my speech therapy, I worried that the Agent Samson plan might work for everyone but me, that the other boys might strengthen their lazy tongues, turn their lives around, and leave me stranded. Luckily my fears were never realized. Despite the woman's best efforts, no one seemed to make any significant improvement. The only difference was that we were all a little quieter. Thanks to Agent Samson's tape recorder, I, along with the others, now had a clear sense of what I actually sounded like. There was the lisp, of course, but more troubling was my voice itself, with its excitable tone and high, girlish pitch. I'd hear myself ordering lunch in the cafeteria, and the sound would turn my stomach. How could anyone stand to listen to me? Whereas those around me might grow up to be lawyers or movie stars, my only option was to take a vow of silence and become a monk. My former classmates would call the abbey, wondering how I was doing, and the priest would answer the phone. "You can't talk to him!" he'd say. "Why, Brother David hasn't spoken to anyone in thirty-five years!"

"Oh, relax," my mother said. "Your voice will change eventually."

"And what if it doesn't?"

She shuddered. "Don't be so morbid."

It turned out that Agent Samson was something along the lines of a circuit-court speech therapist. She spent four months at our school and then moved on to another. Our last meeting was held the day before school let out for Christmas. My classrooms were all decorated, the halls — everything but her office, which remained as bare as ever. I was expecting a regular half hour of Sassy the seal and was delighted to find her packing up her tape recorder.

"I thought that this afternoon we might let loose and have a party, you and I. How does that sound?" She reached into her desk drawer and withdrew a festive tin of cookies. "Here, have one. I made them myself from scratch and, boy, was it a mess! Do you ever make cookies?"

I lied, saying that no, I never had.

"Well, it's hard work," she said. "Especially if you don't have a mixer."

It was unlike Agent Samson to speak so casually, and awkward to sit in the hot little room, pretending to have a normal conversation.

"So," she said, "what are your plans for the holidays?"

"Well, I usually remain here and, you know, open a gift from my family."

"Only one?" she asked.

"Maybe eight or ten."

"Never six or seven?"

"Rarely," I said.

"And what do you do on December thirty-first, New Year's Eve?"

"On the final day of the year we take down the pine tree in our living room and eat marine life."

"You're pretty good at avoiding those s's," she said. "I have to hand it to you, you're tougher than most."

I thought she would continue trying to trip me up, but instead she talked about her own holiday plans. "It's pretty hard with my fiancé in Vietnam," she said. "Last year we went up to see his folks in Roanoke, but this year I'll spend Christmas with my grandmother outside of Asheville. My parents will come, and we'll all try our best to have a good time. I'll eat some turkey and go to church, and then, the next day, a friend and I will drive down to Jacksonville to watch Florida play Tennessee in the Gator Bowl."

I couldn't imagine anything worse than driving down to Florida to watch a football game, but I pretended to be impressed. "Wow, that ought to be eventful."

"I was in Memphis last year when NC State whooped Georgia fourteen to seven in the Liberty Bowl," she said. "And next year, I don't care who's playing, but I want to be sitting front-row center at the Tangerine Bowl. Have you ever been to Orlando? It's a super fun place. If my future husband can find a job in his field, we're hoping to move down there within a year or two. Me living in Florida. I bet that would make you happy, wouldn't it?"

I didn't quite know how to respond. Who was this college bowl fanatic with no mixer and a fiancé in Vietnam, and why had she taken so long to reveal herself? Here I'd thought of her as a cold-blooded agent when she was really nothing but a slightly dopey, inexperienced speech teacher. She wasn't a bad person, Miss Samson, but her timing was off. She should have acted friendly at the beginning of the year instead of waiting until now, when all I could do was feel sorry for her.

"I tried my best to work with you and the others, but sometimes a person's best just isn't good enough." She took another cookie and turned it over in her hands. "I really wanted to prove myself and make a difference in people's lives, but it's hard to do your job when you're met with so much resistance. My students don't like me, and I guess that's just the way it is. What can I say? As a speech teacher, I'm a complete failure."

She moved her hands toward her face, and I worried that she might start to cry. "Hey, look," I said. "I'm thorry."

"Ha-ha," she said. "I got you." She laughed much more than she needed to and was still at it when she signed the form recommending me for the following year's speech therapy program. "Thorry, indeed. You've got some work ahead of you, mister."

I related the story to my mother, who got a huge kick out of it. "You've got to admit that you really are a sucker," she said.

I agreed but, because none of my speech classes ever made a difference, I still prefer to use the word *chump*.

Giant Dreams,

Midget Abilities

My FATHER LOVES JAZZ and has an extensive collection of records and reel-to-reel tapes he used to enjoy after returning home from work. He might have entered the house in a foul mood, but once he had his Dexter Gordon and a vodka martini, the stress melted away and everything was "beautiful, baby, just beautiful." The instant the needle hit that record, he'd loosen his tie and become something other than the conservative engineer with a pocketful of IBM pencils embossed with the command THINK.

"Man, oh man, will you get a load of the chops on this guy? I saw him once at the Blue Note, and I mean to tell you that he blew me right out of my chair! A talent like that comes around only once in a lifetime. The guy was an absolute comet, and there I was in the front row. Can you imagine that?"

"Gee," I'd say, "I bet that was really something."

Empathy was the wrong tack, as it only seemed to irritate him.

"You don't know the half of it," he'd say. " 'Really something,' my butt. You haven't got a clue. You could have taken a hatchet and cut the man's lips right off his face, chopped them off at the quick, and he still would have played better than anyone else out there. That's how good he was."

I'd nod my head, envisioning a pair of glistening lips lying forsaken on the floor of some nightclub dressing room. The trick was to back slowly toward the hallway, escaping into the kitchen before my father could yell, "Oh no you don't. Get back in here. I want you to sit down for a minute and listen. I mean *really* listen, to this next number."

Because it was the music we'd grown up with, I liked to think that my sisters and I had a genuine appreciation of jazz. We preferred it over the music our friends were listening to, yet nothing we did or said could convince my father of our devotion. Aside from replaying the tune on your own instrument, how could you prove you were really listening? It was as if he expected us to change color at the end of each selection.

Due to his ear and his almost maniacal sense of discipline, I always thought my father would have made an excellent musician. He might have studied the saxophone had he not been born to immigrant parents who considered even pot holders an extravagance. They themselves listened only to Greek music, an oxymoron as far as the rest of the world is concerned. Slam its tail in the door of the milk truck, and a stray cat could easily yowl out a single certain to top the charts back in Sparta or Thessaloníki. Jazz was my father's only form of rebellion. It was forbidden in his home, and he appreciated it as though it were his own private discovery. As a young man he hid his 78s under the sofa bed and regularly snuck off to New York City, where he'd haunt the clubs and consort with Negroes. It was a good life while it lasted. He was in his early forties when the company transferred our family to North Carolina.

"You expect me to live *where?*" he'd asked.

The Raleigh winters agreed with him, but he would have gladly traded the temperate climate for a decent radio station. Since he was limited to his record and tape collection, it became his dream that his family might fill the musical void by someday forming a jazz combo.

His plan took shape the evening he escorted my sisters Lisa and Gretchen and me to the local state university to see Dave Brubeck, who was then touring with his sons. The audience roared when the quartet took the stage, and I leaned back and shut my eyes, pretending the applause was for me. In order to get that kind of attention, you needed a routine that would knock people's socks off. I'd been working on something in private and now began to imagine bringing it to a live audience. The act consisted of me, dressed in a nice shirt and tie and singing a medley of commercial jingles in the voice of Billie Holiday, who was one of my father's favorite singers. For my Raleigh concert I'd probably open with the number used to promote the town's oldest shopping center. A quick nod to my accompanist, and I'd launch into "The Excitement of Cameron Village Will Carry You Away." The beauty of my rendition was that it captured both the joy and the sorrow of a visit to Ellisburg's or J. C. Penney. This would be followed by such crowd pleasers as "Winston Tastes Good Like a Cigarette Should" and the catchy new Coke commercial, "I'd Like to Teach the World to Sing."

I was lost in my fantasy, ignoring Dave Brubeck and coming up for air only when my father elbowed my ribs to ask, "Are you *listening* to this? These cats are burning the paint right off the walls!" The other audience members sat calmly, as if in church, while my father snapped his fingers and bobbed his head low against his chest. People pointed, and when we begged him to sit up and act normal, he cupped his hands to his mouth and shouted out a request for " 'Blue Rondo à la Turk'!"

Driving home from the concert that night, he drummed his palms against the steering wheel, saying, "Did you *hear* that? The guy just gets better every day! He's up there onstage with his kids by his side, the whole lot of them jamming up a storm. Christ almighty, what I wouldn't give for a family like that. You guys should think of putting an act together."

My sister Lisa coughed up a mouthful of grapefruit soda.

"No, I mean it," my father said. "All you need are some lessons and instruments, and I swear to God, you'd go right through the roof." We hoped this was just another of his five-minute ideas, but by the time we reached the house, his eyes were still glowing. "That's exactly what you need to do," he said. "I don't know why I didn't think of it sooner."

The following afternoon he bought a baby grand piano. It was a used model that managed to look imposing even when positioned on a linoleum-tiled floor. We took turns stabbing at the keys, but as soon as the novelty wore off, we bolstered it with sofa cushions and turned it into a fort. The piano sat neglected in the traditional sense until my father signed Gretchen up for a series of lessons. She'd never expressed any great interest in the thing but was chosen because, at the age of ten, she possessed what our dad decided were the most artistic fingers. Lisa was assigned the flute, and I returned home from a Scout meeting one evening to find my instrument leaning against the aquarium in my bedroom.

"Hold on to your hat," my father said, "because here's that guitar you've always wanted."

Surely he had me confused with someone else. Although I had regularly petitioned for a brand-name vacuum cleaner, I'd never said anything about wanting a guitar. Nothing about it appealed to me, not even on an aesthetic level. I had my room arranged just so, and the instrument did not fit in with my nautical theme. An anchor, yes. A guitar, no. He wanted me to jam, so I jammed it into my closet, where it remained until he signed me up for some private lessons of-

fered at a music shop located on the ground floor of the recently opened North Hills Mall. I fought it as best I could and
feigned illness even as he dropped me off for my first appointment.

"But I'm sick!" I yelled, watching him pull out of the
parking lot. "I have a virus, and besides that, I don't want to
play a musical instrument. Don't you know *anything?*"

When it finally sank in that he wasn't coming back, I
lugged my guitar into the music store, where the manager
led me to my teacher, a perfectly formed midget named Mister Mancini. I was twelve years old at the time, small for my
age, and it was startling to find myself locked in a windowless
room with a man who barely reached my chest. It seemed
wrong that I would be taller than my teacher, but I kept this
to myself, saying only, "My father told me to come here. It
was all his idea."

A fastidious dresser stuck in a small, unfashionable town,
Mister Mancini wore clothing I recognized from the Young
Squires department of Hudson Belk. Some nights he favored
button-down shirts with clip-on ties, while other evenings I
arrived to find him dressed in flared slacks and snug turtleneck sweaters, a swag of love beads hanging from his neck.
His arms were manly and covered in coarse dark hair, but his
voice was high and strange, as if it had been recorded and
was now being played back at a faster speed.

Not a dwarf, but an honest-to-God midget. My fascina-
tion was both evident and unwelcome, and was nothing he
hadn't been subjected to a million times before. He didn't

shake my hand, just lit a cigarette and reached for the conch shell he used as an ashtray. Like my father, Mister Mancini assumed that anyone could learn to play the guitar. He had picked it up during a single summer spent in what he called "Hotlanta G.A." This, I knew, was the racy name given to Atlanta, Georgia. "Now *that*," he said, "is one classy place if you know where to go." He grabbed my guitar and began tuning it, holding his head close to the strings. "Yes, siree, kid, the girls down on Peachtree are running wild twenty-four hours a day."

He mentioned a woman named Beth, saying, "They threw away the mold and shut down the factory after making that one, you know what I mean?"

I nodded my head, having no idea what he was talking about.

"She wasn't much of a cook, but hey, I guess that's why God invented TV dinners." He laughed at his little joke and repeated the line about the frozen dinners, as if he would use it later in a comedy routine. "God made TV dinners, yeah, that's good." He told me he'd named his guitar after Beth. "Now I can't keep my hands off of her!" he said. "Seriously, though, it helps if you give your instrument a name. What do you think you'll call yours?"

"Maybe I'll call it Oliver," I said. That was the name of my hamster, and I was used to saying it.

Then again, maybe not.

"Oliver?" Mister Mancini set my guitar on the floor.

"*Oliver?* What the hell kind of name is that? If you're going to devote yourself to the guitar, you need to name it after a girl, not a guy."

"Oh, right," I said. "Joan. I'll call it . . . Joan."

"So tell me about this Joan," he said. "Is she something pretty special?"

Joan was the name of one of my cousins, but it seemed unwise to share this information. "Oh yeah," I said, "Joan's really . . . great. She's tall and . . ." I felt self-conscious using the word *tall* and struggled to take it back. "She's small and has brown hair and everything."

"Is she stacked?"

I'd never noticed my cousin's breasts and had lately realized that I'd never noticed anyone's breasts, not unless, like our housekeeper's, they were large enough to appear freakish. "Stacked? Well, sure," I said. "She's pretty stacked." I was afraid he'd ask me for a more detailed description and was relieved when he crossed the room and removed Beth from her case. He told me that a guitar student needed plenty of discipline. Talent was great, but time had taught him that talent was also extremely rare. "I've got it," he said. "But then again, I was born with it. It's a gift from God, and those of us who have it are very special people."

He seemed to know that I was nothing special, just a type, yet another boy whose father had his head in the clouds.

"Do you have a *feel* for the guitar? Do you have any idea

what this little baby is capable of?" Without waiting for an answer, he climbed up into his chair and began playing "Light My Fire," adding, "This one is for Joan.

"'You know that I would be untrue'," he sang. "'You know that I would be a liar'." The current hit version of the song was performed by José Feliciano, a blind man whose plaintive voice served the lyrics much better than did Jim Morrison, who sang it in what I considered a bossy and conceited tone of voice. There was José Feliciano, there was Jim Morrison, and then there was Mister Mancini, who played beautifully but sang "Light My Fire" as if he were a Webelo Scout demanding a match. He finished his opening number, nodded his head in acknowledgment of my applause, and moved on, offering up his own unique and unsettling versions of "The Girl from Ipanema" and "Little Green Apples" while I sat trapped in my seat, my false smile stretched so tight that I lost all feeling in the lower half of my face.

My fingernails had grown a good three inches by the time he struck his final note and called me close to point out a few simple chords. Before I left, he handed me half a dozen purple mimeographed handouts, which we both knew were useless.

Back at the house my mother had my dinner warming in the oven. From the living room came the aimless whisper of Lisa's flute. It sounded not unlike the wind whipping through an empty Pepsi can. Down in the basement either Gretchen was practicing her piano or the cat was chasing a moth across the keys. My mother responded by turning up the volume on the kitchen TV while my father pushed back my plate, set Joan in my lap, and instructed me to play.

"Listen to this," he crowed. "A house full of music! Man, this is beautiful."

You certainly couldn't accuse him of being unsupportive. His enthusiasm bordered on mania, yet still it failed to inspire us. During practice sessions my sisters and I would eat potato chips, scowling at our hated instruments and speculating on the lives of our music teachers. They were all peculiar in one way or another, but with a midget, I'd definitely won the my-teacher-is-stranger-than-yours competition. I wondered where Mister Mancini lived and who he might call in case of an emergency. Did he stand on a chair in order to shave, or was his home customized to meet his needs? I'd look at the laundry hamper or beer cooler, thinking that if it came down to it, Mister Mancini could hide just about anywhere.

Though I thought of him constantly, I grabbed any excuse to avoid my guitar.

"I've been doing just what you told me to do," I'd say at the beginning of each lesson, "but I just can't get the hang of it. Maybe my fingers are too shor — . . . I mean litt — . . . I mean, maybe I'm just not coordinated enough." He'd arrange Joan in my lap, pick up Beth, and tell me to follow along. "You need to believe you're playing an actual woman," he'd say. "Just grab her by the neck and make her holler."

Mr. Mancini had a singular talent for making me uncomfortable. He forced me to consider things I'd rather not think about — the sex of my guitar, for instance. If I honestly wanted to put my hands on a woman, would that automatically mean I could play? Gretchen's teacher never told her to think of her piano as a boy. Neither did Lisa's flute teacher, though in that case the analogy was fairly obvious. On the off chance that sexual desire was all it took, I steered clear of Lisa's instrument, fearing I might be labeled a prodigy. The best solution was to become a singer and leave the instruments to other people. A song stylist — that was what I wanted to be.

I was at the mall with my mother one afternoon when I spotted Mister Mancini ordering a hamburger at Scotty's Chuck Wagon, a fast-food restaurant located a few doors down from the music shop. He sometimes mentioned having lunch with a salesgirl from Jolly's Jewelers, "a real looker," but on this day he was alone. Mister Mancini had to stand on his tiptoes to ask for his hamburger, and even then his head failed to reach the counter. The passing adults politely looked away, but their children were decidedly more vocal. A toddler ambled up on his chubby bowed legs, attempting to embrace my teacher with ketchup-smeared fingers, while a party of elementary-school students openly stared in wonder. Even worse was the group of adolescents, boys my own age, who sat gathered around a large table. "Go back to Oz, munchkin," one of them said, and his friends shook with laughter. Tray in hand, Mister Mancini took a seat and pretended not to notice. The boys weren't yelling, but anyone could tell that they were making fun of him. "Honestly, Mother," I said, "do they have to be such monsters?" Beneath my moral outrage was a strong sense of possessiveness, a fury that other people were sinking their hooks into my own personal midget. What did they know about this man? I was the one who lit his cigarettes and listened as he denounced the careers of so-called pretty boys such as Glen Campbell and Bobby Goldsboro. It was I who had suffered through six weeks' worth of lessons and was still struggling to master "Yellow Bird." If anyone was going to give him a hard time, I figured that I should be first in line.

I'd always thought of Mister Mancini as a blowhard, a pocket playboy, but watching him dip his hamburger into a sad puddle of mayonnaise, I broadened my view and came to see him as a wee outsider, a misfit whose take-it-or-leave-it attitude had left him all alone. This was a persona I'd been tinkering with myself: the outcast, the rebel. It occurred to me that, with the exception of the guitar, he and I actually had quite a bit in common. We were each a man trapped inside a boy's body. Each of us was talented in his own way, and we both hated twelve-year-old males, a demographic group second to none in terms of cruelty. All things considered, there was no reason I shouldn't address him not as a teacher but as an artistic brother. Maybe then we could drop the pretense of Joan and get down to work. If things worked out the way I hoped, I'd someday mention in interviews that my accompanist was both my best friend *and* a midget.

I wore a tie to my next lesson and this time when asked if

I'd practiced, I told the truth, saying in a matter-of-fact tone of voice that no, I hadn't laid a finger on my guitar since our last get-together. I told him that Joan was my cousin's name and that I had no idea how stacked she was.

"That's okay," Mister Mancini said. "You can call your guitar whatever you want, just as long as you practice."

My voice shaking, I told him that I had absolutely no interest in mastering the guitar. What I really wanted was to sing in the voice of Billie Holiday. "Mainly commercials, but not for any banks or car dealerships, because those are usually choral arrangements."

The color ebbed from my teacher's face.

I told him I'd been working up an act and could use a little accompaniment. Did he know the jingle for the new Sara Lee campaign?

"You want me to do what?" He wasn't angry, just confused.

I felt certain he was lying when he denied knowing the tune. Doublemint gum, Ritz crackers, the theme songs for Alka-Seltzer and Kenmore appliances: he claimed ignorance on all counts. I knew that it was queer to sing in front of someone, but greater than my discomfort was the hope that he might recognize what I thought of as my great talent, the one musical trick I was able to pull off. I started in on an a cappella version of the latest Oscar Mayer commercial, hoping he might join in once the spirit moved him. It looked bad, I knew, but in order to sustain the proper mood, I needed to disregard his company and sing the way I did at home alone in my bedroom, my eyes shut tight and my hands dangling like pointless, empty gloves.

I sang that my bologna had a first name.

I added that my bologna had a second name.

And concluded: *Oh, I love to eat it every day*

And if you ask me why, I'll say

Thaaaat Os-carrr May-errr has a way, with B-Oooo-L-Oooo-G-N-A

I reached the end of my tune thinking he might take this as an opportunity to applaud or maybe even apologize for underestimating me. Mild amusement would have been an acceptable response. But instead, he held up his hands, as if to stop an advancing car. "Hey, guy," he said. "You can hold it right there. I'm not into that scene."

A scene? What scene? I thought I was being original.

"There were plenty of screwballs like you back in Atlanta, but me, I don't swing that way — you got it? This might be your 'thing' or whatever, but you can definitely count me out." He reached for his conch shell and stubbed out his cigarette. "I mean, come on now. For God's sake, kid, pull yourself together."

I knew then why I'd never before sung in front of anyone, and why I shouldn't have done it in front of Mister Mancini. He'd used the word *screwball*, but I knew what he really meant. He meant I should have named my guitar Doug or Brian, or better yet, taken up the flute. He meant that if we're defined by our desires, I was in for a lifetime of trouble.

The remainder of the hour was spent awkwardly watching the clock as we silently pretended to tune our guitars.

My father was disappointed when I told him I wouldn't be returning for any more lessons. "He told me not to come back," I said. "He told me I have the wrong kind of fingers."

Seeing that it had worked for me, my sisters invented similar stories, and together we announced that the Sedaris Trio had officially disbanded. Our father offered to find us better teachers, adding that if we were unhappy with our instruments, we could trade them in for something more suitable. "The trumpet or the saxophone, or hey, how about the vibes?" He reached for a Lionel Hampton album, saying, "I want you to sit down and give this a good listen. Just get a load of this cat and tell me he's not an inspiration."

There was a time when I could listen to such a record and imagine myself as the headline act at some magnificent New York nightclub, but that's what fantasies are for: they allow you to skip the degradation and head straight to the top. I'd done my solo and would now move on to pursue other equally unsuccessful ways of getting attention. I'd try every art form there was, and with each disappointment I'd picture Mister Mancini holding his conch shell and saying, "For God's sake, kid, pull yourself together."

We told our father, no, don't bother playing us any more of your records, but still he persisted. "I'm telling you that this album is going to change your lives, and if it doesn't, I'll give each one of you a five-dollar bill. What do you think of that?"

It was a tough call — five dollars for listening to a Lionel Hampton record. The offer was tempting, but even on the off chance he'd actually come through with the money, there would certainly be strings attached. We looked at one another, my sisters and I, and then we left the room, ignoring his cry of "Hey, where do you think you're going? Get back in here and listen."

We joined our mother at the TV and never looked back. A life in music was his great passion, not ours, and our lessons had taught us that without the passion, the best one could hope for was an occasional engagement at some hippie wedding where, if we were lucky, the guests would be too stoned to realize just how bad we really were. That night, as was his habit, our father fell asleep in front of the stereo, the record making its pointless, silent rounds as he lay back against the sofa cushions, dreaming.

Genetic Engineering

My FATHER ALWAYS STRUCK ME as the sort of man who, under the right circumstances, might have invented the microwave oven or the transistor radio. You wouldn't seek him out for advice on a personal problem, but he'd be the first one you'd call when the dishwasher broke or someone flushed a hairpiece down your toilet. As children, we placed a great deal of faith in his ability but learned to steer clear while he was working. The experience of watching was ruined, time and time again, by an interminable explanation of how things were put together. Faced with an exciting question, science tended to provide the dullest possible answer. Ions might charge the air, but they fell flat when it came to charging the imagination — my imagination, anyway. To this day, I prefer to believe that inside every television there lives a community of versatile, thumb-size actors trained to portray everything from a thoughtful newscaster to the wife of a millionaire stranded on a desert island. Fickle gnomes control the weather, and an air conditioner is powered by a team of squirrels, their cheeks packed with ice cubes.

Once, while rifling through the toolshed, I came across a poster advertising an IBM computer the size of a refrigerator. Sitting at the control board was my dad the engineer, years younger, examining a printout no larger than a grocery receipt. When I asked about it, he explained that he had worked with a team devising a memory chip capable of storing up to fifteen pages' worth of information. Out came the notepad and pencil, and I was trapped for hours as he answered every question except the one I had asked: "Were you allowed to wear makeup and run through a variety of different poses, or did they get the picture on the first take?"

To me, the greatest mystery of science continues to be that a man could father six children who shared absolutely none of his interests. We certainly expressed enthusiasm for our mother's hobbies, from smoking and napping to the writings of Sidney Sheldon. (Ask my mother how the radio worked and her answer was simple: "Turn it on and pull out the goddamn antenna.") I once visited my father's office, and walked away comforted to find that at least there he had a few people he could talk to. We'd gone, my sister Amy and I, to settle a bet. She thought that my father's secretary had a sharp, protruding chin and long blond hair, while I imagined that the woman might more closely resemble a tortoise —

chinless, with a beaky nose and a loose, sagging neck. The correct answer was somewhere in between. I was right about the nose and the neck, but Amy won on the chin and the hair color. The bet had been the sole reason for our visit, and the resulting insufferable tour of Buildings A through D taught us never again to express an interest in our father's workplace.

My own scientific curiosity eventually blossomed, but I knew enough to keep my freakish experiments to myself. When my father discovered my colony of frozen slugs in the basement freezer, I chose not to explain my complex theories of suspended animation. Why was I filling the hamster's water beaker with vodka? "Oh, no reason." If my experiment failed, and the drunken hamster passed out, I'd just put her in the deep freeze, alongside the slugs. She'd rest on ice for a few months and, once thawed and fully revived, would remember nothing of her previous life as an alcoholic. I also took to repairing my own record-player and was astonished by my ingenuity for up to ten minutes at a time — until the rubber band snapped or the handful of change came unglued from the arm, and the damned thing broke all over again.

During the first week of September, it was my family's habit to rent a beach house on Ocean Isle, a thin strip of land off the coast of North Carolina. As youngsters, we participated in all the usual seaside activities — which were fun, until my father got involved and systematically chipped away at our pleasure. Miniature golf was ruined with a lengthy dissertation on impact, trajectory, and wind velocity, and our sand castles were critiqued with stifling lectures on the dynamics of the vaulted ceiling. We enjoyed swimming, until the mystery of tides was explained in such a way that the ocean seemed nothing more than an enormous saltwater toilet, flushing itself on a sad and predictable basis.

By the time we reached our teens, we were exhausted. No longer interested in the water, we joined our mother on the beach blanket and dedicated ourselves to the higher art of tanning. Under her guidance, we learned which lotions to start off with, and what worked best for various weather conditions and times of day. She taught us that the combination of false confidence and Hawaiian Tropic could result in a painful and unsightly burn, certain to subtract valuable points when, on the final night of vacation, contestants gathered for the annual Miss Emollient Pageant. This was a contest judged by our mother, in which the holder of the darkest tan was awarded a crown, a sash, and a scepter.

Technically, the prize could go to either a male or a female, but the sash read MISS EMOLLIENT because it was always assumed that my sister Gretchen would once again sweep the title. For her, tanning had moved from an intense hobby to something more closely resembling a psychological dysfunction. She was what we called a tanorexic: someone who simply could not get enough. Year after year she arrived at the beach with a base coat that the rest of us could only dream of achieving as our final product. With a mixture of awe and envy, we watched her broiling away on her aluminum blanket. The spaces between her toes were tanned, as were her palms and even the backs of her ears. Her method involved baby oil and a series of poses that tended to draw crowds, the mothers shielding their children's eyes with sand-covered fingers.

It is difficult for me to sit still for more than twenty minutes at a stretch, so I used to interrupt my tanning sessions with walks to the pier. On one of those walks, I came across my father standing not far from a group of fishermen who were untangling knots in a net the size of a circus tent. A lifetime of work beneath the coastal sun had left them with what my sisters and I referred to as the Samsonite Syndrome, meaning that their enviable color was negated by a hard, leathery texture reminiscent of the suitcase my mother stored all our baby pictures in. The men drank from quart bottles of Mountain Dew as they paused from their work to regard my father, who stood at the water's edge, staring at the shoreline with a stick in his hand.

I tried to creep by unnoticed, but he stopped me, claiming that I was just the fellow he'd been looking for. "Do you have any idea how many grains of sand there are in the world?" he asked. It was a question that had never occurred to me. Unlike guessing the number of pickled eggs in a jar or the amount of human brains it might take to equal the weight of a portable television set, this equation was bound to involve the hateful word *googolplex,* a term I'd heard him use once or twice before. It was an *idea* of a number and was, therefore, of no use whatsoever.

I'd heard once in school that if a single bird were to transport all the sand, grain by grain, from the eastern seaboard to the west coast of Africa, it would take . . . I didn't catch the number of years, preferring to concentrate on the single bird chosen to perform this thankless task. It hardly seemed fair, because, unlike a horse or a Seeing Eye dog, the whole glory of being a bird is that nobody would ever put you to work. Birds search for grubs and build their nests, but their leisure time is theirs to spend as they see fit. I pictured this bird looking down from the branches to say, "You want me to do what?" before flying off, laughing at the foolish story he now had to tell his friends. How many grains of sand are there in the world? A lot. Case closed.

My father took his stick and began writing an equation in the sand. Like all the rest of them, this one was busy with x's and y's resting on top of one another on dash-shaped bunks. Letters were multiplied by symbols, crowded into parentheses, and set upon by dwarfish numbers drawn at odd angles. The equation grew from six to twelve feet long before assuming a second line, at which point the fishermen took an interest. I watched them turn from their net, and admired the way they could smoke entire cigarettes without ever taking them from their mouths — a skill my mother had mastered and one that continues to elude me. It involves a symbiotic relationship with the wind: you have to know exactly how and when to turn your head in order to keep the smoke out of your eyes.

One of the men asked my father if he was a tax accountant, and he answered, "No, an engineer." These were poor men, who could no longer afford to live by the ocean, who had long ago sold their one-story homes for the valuable sand beneath them. Their houses had been torn down to make room for high-priced hotels and the A-frame cottages that now rented in season for a thousand dollars a week.

"Let me ask a little something," one of the men said, spitting his spent cigarette butt into the surf. "If I got paid twelve thousand dollars in 1962 for a half-acre beachfront lot, how much would that be worth per grain of sand by today's standard?"

"That, my friend, is a very interesting question," my father said.

He moved several yards down the beach and began a new equation, captivating his audience with a lengthy explanation of each new and complex symbol. "When you say *pie*," one man asked, "do you mean a real live pie, or one of those pie shapes they put on the news sometimes to show how much of your money goes to taxes?"

My father answered their questions in detail, and they listened intently — this group of men with nets, blowing their smoke into the wind. Stooped and toothless, they hung upon his every word while I stood in the lazy surf, thinking of the upcoming pageant and wondering if the light reflecting off the water might tan the underside of my nose and chin.

Twelve Moments
in the Life of the Artist

One: At an early age my sister Gretchen exhibited a remarkable talent for drawing and painting. Her watercolors of speckled mushrooms and bonneted girls were hung with pride in the family room, and her skill was encouraged with private lessons and summer visits to sketching camp. Born with what my mother defined as an "artistic temperament," Gretchen floated from blossom to blossom in a blissful haze. Staring dreamily up at the sky, she tripped over logs and stepped out in front of speeding bicycles. When the casts were placed on her arms and legs, she personalized them with Magic Marker daisies and fluffy clouds. Physically she'd been stitched up more times than the original flag, but mentally nothing seemed to touch her. You could tell Gretchen anything in strict confidence, knowing that five minutes later she would recall nothing but the play of shadows on your face. It was like having a foreign-exchange student living in our house. Nothing we did or said made any sense to her, as she seemed to follow the rules and customs of some exotic, faraway nation where the citizens drilled the ground for oil paint and picked pastels from the branches of stunted trees. Without copying anyone else, she had invented her own curious personality, which I envied even more than her artistic ability.

When Gretchen's talent was recognized by teachers, both my parents stepped forward to claim responsibility. As a child my mother had shown a tendency for drawing and mud sculpture and could still amuse us with her speedy re-creations of a popular cartoon woodpecker. Proving his to be a latent gift, my father bought himself a box of acrylic paints and set up his easel in front of the basement TV, turning out exact copies of Renoir cafés and Spanish monks brooding beneath their hooded robes. He painted New York streetscapes and stagecoaches riding into fiery sunsets — and then, once he'd filled the basement walls with his efforts, he stopped painting as mysteriously as he'd begun. It seemed to me that if my father could be an artist, anyone could. Snatching up his palette and brushes, I retreated to my bedroom, where, at the age of fourteen, I began my long and disgraceful blue period.

Two: When painting proved too difficult, I turned to tracing comic-book characters on to onionskin typing paper, telling myself that I would have come up with Mr. Natural on my own had I been born a few years earlier. The main thing was to stay focused and provide myself with realistic goals. Unlike my father, who blindly churned out one canvas after another, I had real ideas about the artistic life. Seated at my desk, my beret as tight as an acorn's cap, I projected myself into the world represented in the art books I'd borrowed from the public library. Leafing past the paintings, I would admire the photographs of the artists seated in their garrets, dressed in tattered smocks and frowning in the direction of their beefy nude models. To spend your days in the company of naked men — that was the life for me. "Turn a bit to the left, Jean-Claude. I long to capture the playful quality of your buttocks."

I envisioned the finicky curators coming to my door and begging me to hold another show at the Louvre or the Metropolitan. After a lunch of white wine and tongue-size cutlets, we would retire to the gentlemen's lounge and talk about money. I could clearly see the results of my labor: the long satin scarves and magazine covers were very real to me. What I couldn't begin to imagine was the artwork itself. The only crimp in my plan was that I seemed to have no talent whatsoever. This was made clear when I signed up for art classes in high school. Asked to render a bowl of grapes, I would turn in what resembled a pile of stones hovering above a whitewall tire. My sister's paintings were prominently displayed on the walls of the classroom, and the teacher invoked her name whenever discussing perspective or color. She was included in all the city- and countywide shows and never mentioned the blue ribbons scotch-taped to her entries. Had she been a braggart, it would have been much easier to hate her. As it was, I had to wrestle daily with both my inadequacy and my uncontrollable jealousy. I didn't want to kill her, but hoped someone else might do the job for me.

Three: Away from home and the inevitable comparisons with Gretchen, I enrolled as an art major at a college known mainly for its animal-husbandry program. The night before my first life-drawing class, I lay awake worrying that I might get physically excited by the nude models. Here would be this person, hopefully a strapping animal-husbandry major, displaying his tanned and muscled body before an audience of students who, with the exception of me, would see him as nothing but an armature of skin and bones. Would the teacher take note of my bulging eyes or comment on the thin strand of saliva hanging like fishing wire from the corner of my mouth? Could I skip the difficult hands and feet and just concentrate on the parts that interested me, or would I be forced to sketch the entire figure?

My fears were genuine but misplaced. Yes, the model was beefy and masculine, but she was also a woman. Staring too hard was never an issue, as I was too busy trying to copy my neighbor's drawings. The teacher made his rounds from easel to easel, and I monitored his progress with growing panic.

Maybe he didn't know my sister, but there were still plenty of other talented students to compare me with.

Frustrated with drawing, I switched to the printmaking department, where I overturned great buckets of ink. After trying my hand at sculpture, I attempted pottery. During class critiques the teacher would lift my latest project from the table and I'd watch her arm muscles strain and tighten against the weight. With their thick, clumsy bases, my mugs weighed in at close to five pounds each. The color was muddy and the lips rough and uninviting. I gave my mother a matching set for Christmas, and she accepted them as graciously as possible, announcing that they would make the perfect pet bowls. The mugs were set on the kitchen floor and remained there until the cat chipped a tooth and went on a hunger strike.

Four: I transferred to another college and started the whole humiliating process all over again. After switching from lithography to clay modeling, I stopped attending classes altogether, preferring to concentrate on what my roommate and I referred to as the "Bong Studies Program." A new set of owlish glasses made pinpoints of my red-rimmed eyes, and I fell in with a crowd of lazy filmmakers who talked big but wound up spending their production allowances on gummy bricks of hash. In their company I attended grainy black-and-white movies in which ponderous, turtlenecked men slogged the stony beaches, cursing the gulls for their ability to fly. The camera would cut to a field of ragged crows and then to a freckle-faced woman who sat in a sunbeam examining her knuckles. It was all I could do to stay awake until the movie ended and I could file out of the theater behind the melancholy ticketholders, who bore a remarkable resemblance to the pale worrywarts I'd seen flickering up on the screen. True art was based upon despair, and the important thing was to make yourself and those around you as miserable as possible. Maybe I couldn't paint or sculpt, but I could work a mood better than anyone I knew. Unfortunately, the school had no accredited sulking program and I dropped out, more despondent than ever.

Five: My sister Gretchen was leaving for the Rhode Island School of Design just as I was settling back into Raleigh. After a few months in my parents' basement, I took an apartment near the state university, where I discovered both crystal methamphetamine and conceptual art. Either one of these things is dangerous, but in combination they have the potential to destroy entire civilizations. The moment I took my first burning snootful, I understood that this was the drug for me. Speed eliminates all doubt. Am I smart enough? Will people like me? Do I really look all right in this plastic jumpsuit? These are questions for insecure potheads. A speed enthusiast knows that everything he says or does is brilliant.

The upswing is that, having eliminated the need for both eating and sleeping, you have a full twenty-four hours a day to spread your charm and talent.

"For God's sake," my father would say, "it's two o'clock in the morning. What are you calling for?"

I was calling because the rest of my friends had taken to unplugging their phones after ten P.M. These were people I'd known in high school, and it disappointed me to see how little we now had in common. They were still talking about pen-and-ink portraits and couldn't understand my desire to drag a heavy cash register through the forest. I hadn't actually *done* it, but it sounded like a good idea to me. These people were all stuck in the past, setting up their booths at the art fair and thinking themselves successful because they'd sold a silk screen of a footprint in the sand. It was sad in a way. Here they were, struggling to make art, while without the least bit of effort, I was *living* art. My socks balled up on the hardwood floor made a greater statement than any of their hokey claptrap with the carefully matted frames and big curly signatures in the lower left-hand corners. Didn't they read any of the magazines? The new breed of artist wanted nothing to do with my sister's idea of beauty. Here were people who made a living pitching tents or lying in a fetal position before our national monuments. One fellow had made a name for himself by allowing a friend to shoot him in the shoulder. This was the art world I'd been dreaming of, where God-given talent was considered an unfair advantage and a cold-blooded stare merited more praise than the ability to render human flesh. Everything around me was art, from the stains in my bathtub to the razor blade and short length of drinking straw I used to cut and ingest my speed. I was back in the world with a clear head and a keen vision of just how talented I really was.

"Let me put your mother on," my father would say. "She's had a few drinks, so maybe she can understand whatever the hell it is you're talking about."

Six: I bought my drugs from a jittery, bug-eyed typesetter whose brittle, prematurely white hair was permed in such a way that I couldn't look at her without thinking of a late-season dandelion. Selling me the drugs was no problem, but listening to my increasingly manic thoughts and opinions was far too much for one person to take on a daily basis.

"I'm thinking of parceling off portions of my brain," I once told her. "I'm not talking about having anything surgically removed, I'd just like to divide it into lots and lease it out so that people could say, 'I've got a house in Raleigh, a cottage in Myrtle Beach, and a little hideaway inside a visionary's head.'"

Her bored expression suggested the questionable value of my mental real estate. Speed heats the brain to a full boil, leaving the mouth to function as a fulminating exhaust pipe. I talked until my tongue bled, my jaw gave out, and my throat swelled up in protest.

Hoping to get me off her back, my dealer introduced me to half a dozen hyperactive brainiacs who shared my taste for amphetamines and love of the word *manifesto*. Here, finally, was my group. The first meeting was tense, but I broke the ice by laying out a few lines of crystal and commenting on my host's refreshing lack of furniture. His living room contained nothing but an enormous nest made of human hair. It seemed that he drove twice a week to all the local beauty parlors and barbershops, collecting their sweepings and arranging them, strand by strand, as carefully as a wren.

"I've been building this nest for, oh, about six months now," he said. "Go ahead, have a seat."

Other group members stored their bodily fluids in baby-food jars or wrote cryptic messages on packaged cheap steaks. Their artworks were known as "pieces," a phrase I enthusiastically embraced. "Nice piece," I'd say. In my eagerness to please, I accidentally complimented chipped baseboards and sacks of laundry waiting to be taken to the cleaners. Anything might be a piece if you looked at it hard enough. High on crystal, the gang and I would tool down the beltway, admiring the traffic cones and bright yellow speed bumps. The art world was our conceptual oyster, and we ate it raw.

Inspired by my friends, I undertook a few pieces of my own. My first project was a series of wooden vegetable crates I meticulously filled with my garbage. Seeing as how I no longer ate anything, there were no rotting food scraps to worry about, just cigarette butts, aspirin tins, wads of under-nourished hair, and bloody Kleenex. Because these were pieces, I carefully recorded each entry using an ink I'd made from the crushed bodies of ticks and mosquitoes.

2:17 A.M.: Four toenail clippings.

3:48 A.M.: Eyelash discovered beside sink. Moth.

Once the first two crates were completed, I carried them down to the art museum for consideration in their upcoming juried biennial. When the notice arrived that my work had been accepted, I foolishly phoned my friends with the news. Their proposals to set fire to the grand staircase or sculpt the governor's head out of human feces had all been rejected. This officially confirmed their outsider status and made me an enemy of the avant-garde. At the next group meeting it was suggested that the museum had accepted my work only because it was decorative and easy to swallow. My friends could have gotten in had they compromised themselves, but unlike me, some people had integrity.

Plans were made for an alternative exhibit, and I wound up attending the museum opening in the company of my mother and my drug dealer, who by this time had lost so much hair and weight that, in her earth-tone sheath, she resembled a cocktail onion speared on a toothpick. The two of them made quite a pair, hogging the wet bar and loudly sharing their uninformed opinions with anyone within earshot. There was a little jazz combo playing in the corner, and the waiters circulated with trays of jumbo shrimp and stuffed mushrooms. I observed the crowd gathered around my crates, wanting to overhear their comments but feeling a deeper need to keep tabs on my mother. I looked over at one point and caught her drunkenly clutching the arm of the curator, shouting, "I just passed a lady in the bathroom and told her, 'Honey, why flush it? Carry it into the next room and they'll put it on a goddamn pedestal.' "

Seven: I told my friends that I had hated every moment of the museum reception, which was practically true. The show was up for two months, and when it came down, I carried my crates to a vacant lot and burned them in penitence for my undeserved success. I had paid for my folly and, as a reward, was invited to take part in the nest builder's performance piece. The script was great.

"When I bleat here on page seventeen, do you want me to just bleat or to really let go and 'bleat, bleat'? " I asked. "I feel like 'bleat, bleating,' but if Mother/Destroyer is going to be crawling through the birth canal of concertina wire, I don't want to steal focus, you know what I mean?"

He did. That was the scary part, that someone understood me. It occurred to me that a performance piece was something like a play. A play without a story, dialogue, or any discernible characters. That kind of a play. I was enchanted.

We found ourselves a raw space, and oh, how I loved the way those words tripped off my tongue. "We've located a great raw space for the piece," I'd tell my outside friends. "It's an abandoned tobacco warehouse with no running water or electricity. It's got to be a good hundred and twenty degrees in there! You really ought to come down and see the show. There are tons of fleas, and it's going to be really deep."

My parents attended the premiere, sitting cross-legged on one of the padded mats spread like islands across the filthy concrete floor. Asked later what she thought of the performance, my mother massaged her knees, asking, "Are you trying to punish me for something?"

The evening newspaper ran a review headlined LOCAL GROUP PITCHES IN, CLEANS UP WAREHOUSE. This did nothing to encourage the ticket buyers, whose numbers dwindled to the single digits by the second night of our weeklong run. Word of mouth hurt us even more, but we comforted ourselves by blaming a population so brainwashed by television that they couldn't sit through a simple two-and-a-half-hour performance piece without complaining of boredom and leg cramps. We were clearly ahead of our time but figured that, with enough drugs, the citizens of North Carolina would eventually catch up with us.

Eight: The nest builder announced plans for his next performance piece, and the group fell apart. "Why is it always *your* piece?" we asked. As leader, it was his fate to be punished for having the very qualities we admired in the first place. His charisma, his genuine commitment, even his nest — all these things became suspect. When he offered us the opportunity to create our own roles, we became even angrier. Who was *he* to give assignments and set deadlines? We lacked the ability to think for ourselves and resented having to admit it. This led to an epic shouting match in which we exhausted all our analogies and then started all over again from the top. "We're not your puppets or little trained dogs, willing to jump through some hoop. What, do you think we're puppets? Do we look like puppets to you? We're not puppets *or* dogs, and we're not going to jump through any more of your hoops, Puppet Master. Oh, you can train a dog. Stick your hand up a puppet's ass and he'll pretty much do whatever you want him to, but we're not playing that game anymore, Herr Puppet Meister. We're through playing your tricks, so find someone else."

I had hoped that the group might stay together forever, but within ten minutes it was all over, finished, with each of us vowing to perform only our own work. I spent the next several weeks running the argument over and over in my mind, picturing a small dog chasing a puppet across the floor of an abandoned warehouse. How could I have been so stupid as to throw away the only opportunity I'd ever have?

I was at home braiding the bristles on my whisk broom when the museum called, inviting me to participate in their new "Month of Sundays" performance-art festival. It seemed as though I should play hard to get, but after a moment or two of awkward silence, I agreed to do it for what I called "political reasons." I needed the money for drugs.

Nine: Watching the performances of my former colleagues, I got the idea that once you assembled the requisite props, the piece would more or less come together on its own. The inflatable shark naturally led to the puddle of heavy cream, which, if lapped from the floor with slow, steady precision, could account for up to twenty minutes of valuable stage time. All you had to do was maintain a shell-shocked expression and handle a variety of contradictory objects. It was the artist's duty to find the appropriate objects, and the audience's job to decipher meaning. If the piece failed to work, it was their fault, not yours.

My search for the appropriate objects led me to a secondhand store. Standing at the checkout counter with an armload of sock monkeys, I told the cashier, "These are for a piece I'm working on. It's a performance commissioned by the art museum. I'm an artist."

"Really?" The woman stabbed her cigarette into a bucketful of sand. "My niece is an artist, too! She's the one who made those sock monkeys."

"Yes," I said. "But I'm a *real* artist."

The woman was not offended, only puzzled. "But my niece lives over in Winston-Salem." She said it as if living in Winston-Salem automatically signified an artistic temperament. "She's a big, blond-headed girl with twin babies just about grown. Everybody calls her the sock lady on account of that she's always making those monkeys. She's a pretty girl, big-boned but just as talented as she can be."

I looked into this woman's face, her fuzzy jowls hanging like saddlebags, and I pictured her reclining nude in a shallow pool of peanut oil. Were she smart enough to let me, I could use her as my living prop. I could be the best thing that ever happened to her, but sadly, she was probably too ignorant to appreciate it. Maybe one day I'd do a full-length piece on the topic of stupidity, but in the meantime, I'd just pay for the sock monkeys, snort a few lines of speed, and finish constructing a bulletproof vest out of used flashlight batteries.

Ten: Quite a few people showed up for the museum performance, and I stood before them wishing they were half as high as I was. I'd been up for close to three days and had taken so much speed that I could practically see the individual atoms pitching in to make up every folding chair. *Why is everyone staring at me?* I wondered. *Don't they have anything better to do?* I thought I was just being paranoid, and then I remembered that I was being stared at for a reason. I was onstage, and everyone else was in the audience, waiting for me to do something meaningful. The show wasn't over. It had only just begun. I reminded myself that this was my moment. All I had to do was open my prop box, and the rest of the piece would take care of itself.

I'm slicing this pineapple now, I thought. *Next I'll just rip apart these sock monkeys and pour the stuffing into this tall rubber boot. Good, that's good. Nobody pours stuffing like you do, my friend. Now I'll snip off some of my hair with these garden shears, place the bottlecaps over my eyes, and we're almost home.*

I moved toward the audience and was kneeling in the aisle, the shears to my head, when I heard someone say, "Just take a little off the back and sides."

It was my father, speaking in a loud voice to the woman seated beside him.

"Hey, sport," he called, "what do you charge for a shave?"

The audience began to laugh and enjoy themselves.

"He should probably open a barbershop, because he's sure not going anywhere in the show-business world."

It was *him* again, and once more the audience laughed. I was spitting tacks, trying my hardest to concentrate but thinking, *Doesn't he see the Botticelli hanging on the wall behind me? Has he no idea how to behave in an art museum? This is my work, damn it. This is what I do, and here he's treating it like some kind of a joke. You are a dead man, Lou Sedaris. And I'll see to that personally.*

Immediately following the performance a small crowd gathered around my father, congratulating him on his delivery and comic timing.

"Including your father was an excellent idea," the curator said, handing me my check. "The piece really came together once you loosened up and started making fun of yourself."

Not only did my father ask for a cut of the money, but he also started calling with suggestions for future pieces. "What if you were to symbolize man's inhumanity to man by heating up a skillet of plastic soldiers?"

I told him that was the cheesiest idea I'd ever heard in my

life and asked him to stop calling me with his empty little propositions. "I'm an artist!" I yelled. "I come up with the ideas. *Me,* not you. This isn't some party game, it's serious work, and I'd rather stick a gun to my head than listen to any more of your bullshit suggestions."

There was a brief pause before he said, "The bit with the gun just might work. Let me think about it and get back to you."

Eleven: My performing career effectively ended the day my drug dealer moved to Georgia to enter a treatment center. Since the museum I'd done a piece at a gallery and had another scheduled for the state university. "How can you do this to me?" I asked her. "You can't move away, not now. Think of all the money I've spent on you. Don't I deserve more than a week's notice? And what do you need with a treatment center? People like you the way you are; what makes you think you need to change? Just cut back a little, and you'll be fine. Please, you can't do this to me. I have a piece to finish, goddamnit. I'm an artist and I need to know where my drugs are coming from."

Nothing I said would change her mind. I cashed in a savings bond left to me by my grandmother and used the money to buy what I hoped would be enough speed to get me through the month. It was gone in ten days, and with it went my ability to do anything but roll on the floor and cry. It would have made for a decent piece, but I couldn't think about that at the time.

Speed's breathtaking high is followed by a crushing, suicidal depression. You're forced to pay tenfold for all the fun you thought you were having. It's torturous and demeaning, yet all you can think is that you want more. I might have thrown myself out the window, but I lived on the first floor and didn't have the energy to climb the stairs to the roof. Everything ached, and even without the speed I was unable to sleep. Thinking I must have dropped a grain or two, I vacuumed the entire apartment with a straw up my nose, sucking up dead skin cells, Comet residue, and pulverized cat litter. Anything that traveled on the bottom of a shoe went up my nose.

A week after my drugs ran out, I left my bed to perform at the college, deciding at the last minute to skip both the doughnut toss and the march of the headless plush toys. Instead, I just heated up a skillet of plastic soldiers, poured a milkshake over my head, and called it a night.

A few of my former friends showed up at the performance, looking just as sweaty and desperate as I did. Following the piece, they invited themselves to my apartment and I welcomed them, hoping that somebody still had some drugs. It turned out that they were thinking the exact same thing. We sat around making small talk and watching one another's hands. Someone would reach into his pocket and we'd all perk up until the hand returned bearing nothing but a cigarette. The shame was nothing I ever could have conveyed with thimbles or squirt guns filled with mayonnaise. A fistful of burning hair could not begin to represent the mess I had made of my life.

I thought briefly of checking myself into a hospital, but I'd seen what those wards looked like and I've always hated having a roommate. Perhaps this was something that with hard work and determination I could overcome. Maybe I could sober up, get my personal life in order, and reevaluate my priorities. Chances were that I had no artistic talent whatsoever. If I were to face that fact, possibly I could move on with my life, maybe learn a trade and take pride in my ability to shingle roofs or knock the dents out of cars. There was no shame in working with your hands and returning home at night to a glass of ice water and the satisfaction that you'd brightened someone's afternoon with a pock-free fender. Lots of people did things like that. You might not read their names in the magazines, but still they were out there, day after day, giving it all they had. Better yet, I decided — at the age of twenty-seven — to return to art school. They'd have plenty of drugs there.

Twelve: I take my seat on the cold concrete floor, watching as a full-grown woman kneels before an altar made of fudge. She's already put away a gingerbread cabin, two pints of ice cream, and a brood of marshmallow chicks — all without saying a word. The effect is excruciating, but I have no one but myself to blame. I find myself attending these performance pieces the same way certain friends drop by their

AA meetings. I still do a lot of selfish and terrible things. I do not, however, treat myself to hot-cocoa enemas before an audience of invited guests. Minor as it seems, this has become something to celebrate.

The woman onstage has tottered on stilts fashioned from empty cans of Slim-Fast. She's taken her eating disorder on the road, conditioning her hair with whipped topping and rolling her bangs in finger-size breakfast sausages. Just when I think she's finished with all her props and is ready to toss up an ending, out comes a bust of Venus made from cake frosting. Looking around, I notice my fellow audience members examining their cuticles and staring with great purpose at the exit sign. Like me, they're thinking of something positive to say once the spectacle is over and the performer takes up her post beside the front door. The obvious comment would come in the form of a question, that being, "What in God's name possessed you to do such a thing, and why is it that nobody stopped you?" I'm not here to cause trouble, so it's probably best to remark upon a single detail. When the time comes, I take her sticky hand in mine and ask how she manages to keep her frosting so stiff. This is neither damning nor encouraging. It is simply my password out on to the street, where I can embrace life with a renewed sense of liberty. The girl standing in front of the delicatessen stoops to tie her shoe. I watch as farther down the block a white-haired man tosses a business card into the trash. I turn for a moment at the sound of a car alarm and then continue along my way, unencumbered. No one expects me to applaud or consider the relationship between the shoelace and the white-haired man. The car alarm is not a metaphor, but just an unrehearsed annoyance. This is a new and brighter world, in which I am free to hurry along, celebrating my remarkable ability to walk, to run.

You Can't
Kill the Rooster

WHEN I WAS YOUNG, my father was transferred and our family moved from western New York State to Raleigh, North Carolina. IBM had relocated a great many northerners, and together we made relentless fun of our new neighbors and their poky, backward way of life. Rumors circulated that the locals ran stills out of their toolsheds and referred to their house cats as "good eatin'." Our parents discouraged us from using the titles "ma'am" or "sir" when addressing a teacher or shopkeeper. Tobacco was acceptable in the form of a cigarette, but should any of us experiment with plug or snuff, we would automatically be disinherited. Mountain Dew was forbidden, and our speech was monitored for the slightest hint of a Raleigh accent. Use the word "y'all," and before you knew it, you'd find yourself in a haystack French-kissing an underage goat. Along with grits and hush puppies, the abbreviated form of *you all* was a dangerous step on an insidious path leading straight to the doors of the Baptist church.

We might not have been the wealthiest people in town, but at least we weren't one of *them*.

Our family remained free from outside influence until 1968, when my mother gave birth to my brother, Paul, a North Carolina native who has since grown to become both my father's best ally and worst nightmare. Here was a child who, by the time he had reached the second grade, spoke much like the toothless fishermen casting their nets into Albemarle Sound. This is the grown man who now phones his father to say, "Motherfucker, I ain't seen pussy in so long, I'd throw stones at it."

My brother's voice, like my own, is high-pitched and girlish. Telephone solicitors frequently ask to speak to our husbands or request that we put our mommies on the line. The Raleigh accent is soft and beautifully cadenced, but my brother's is a more complex hybrid, informed by his professional relationships with marble-mouthed, deep-country work crews and his abiding love of hard-core rap music. He talks so fast that even his friends have a hard time understanding him. It's like listening to a foreigner and deciphering only *shit, motherfucker, bitch,* and the single phrase *You can't kill the Rooster.*

"The Rooster" is what Paul calls himself when he's feeling threatened. Asked how he came up with that name, he says only, "Certain motherfuckers think they can fuck with my shit, but you can't kill the Rooster. You might can fuck him up sometimes, but, bitch, nobody kills the motherfucking Rooster. You know what I'm saying?"

It often seems that my brother and I were raised in two completely different households. He's eleven years younger than I am, and by the time he reached high school, the rest of us had all left home. When I was young, we weren't allowed to say "shut up," but once the Rooster hit puberty it had become acceptable to shout, "Shut your motherfucking hole." The drug laws had changed as well. "No smoking pot" became "no smoking pot in the house," before it finally petered out to "please don't smoke any more pot in the living room."

My mother was, for the most part, delighted with my brother and regarded him with the bemused curiosity of a brood hen discovering she has hatched a completely different species. "I think it was very nice of Paul to give me this vase," she once said, arranging a bouquet of wildflowers into the skull-shaped bong my brother had left on the dining-room table. "It's nontraditional, but that's the Rooster's way. He's a free spirit, and we're lucky to have him."

Like most everyone else in our suburban neighborhood, we were raised to meet a certain standard. My father expected me to attend an Ivy League university, where I'd make straight A's, play football, and spend my off-hours strumming guitar with the student jazz combo. My inability to throw a football was exceeded only by my inability to master the gui-

tar. My grades were average at best, and eventually I learned
to live with my father's disappointment. Fortunately there
were six of us children, and it was easy to get lost in the
crowd. My sisters and I managed to sneak beneath the wire of
his expectations, but we worried about my brother, who was
seen as the family's last hope.

From the age of ten, Paul was being dressed in Brooks
Brothers suits and tiny, clip-on rep ties. He endured trumpet
lessons, soccer camp, church-sponsored basketball tourna-
ments, and after-school sessions with well-meaning tutors
who would politely change the subject when asked about the
Rooster's chances of getting into Yale or Princeton. Fast and
well-coordinated, Paul enjoyed sports but not enough to take
them seriously. School failed to interest him on any level, and
the neighbors were greatly relieved when he finally retired
his trumpet. His response to our father's impossible and endless demands has, over time, become something of a mantra.
Short and sweet, repeated at a fever pitch, it goes simply,
"Fuck it," or on one of his more articulate days, "Fuck it,
motherfucker. That shit don't mean fuck to me."

My brother politely ma'ams and sirs all strangers but
refers to friends and family, his father included, as either
"bitch" or "motherfucker." Friends are appalled at the way he
speaks to his only remaining parent. The two of them once
visited my sister Amy and me in New York City, and we celebrated with a dinner party. When my father complained
about his aching feet, the Rooster set down his two-liter

bottle of Mountain Dew and removed a fistful of prime rib from his mouth, saying, "Bitch, you need to have them ugly-ass bunions shaved down is what you need to do. But you can't do shit about it tonight, so lighten up, motherfucker."

All eyes went to my father, who chuckled, saying only, "Well, I guess you have a point."

A stranger might reasonably interpret my brother's language as a lack of respect and view my father's response as a form of shameful surrender. This, though, would be missing the subtle beauty of their relationship.

My father is the type who once recited a bawdy limerick, saying, "A woman I know who's quite blunt / had a bear trap installed in her . . . Oh, you know. It's a base, vernacular word for the vagina." He can absolutely kill a joke. When pushed to his limit, this is a man who shouts, "Fudge," a man who curses drivers with a shake of his fist and a hearty "G.D. you!" I've never known him to swear, yet he and my brother seem to have found a common language that eludes the rest of us.

My father likes to talk about money. Spending doesn't interest him in the least, especially as he grows older. He prefers money as a concept and often uses terms such as *annuity* and *fiduciary*, words definitely not listed in the dictionary of mindless entertainment. It puts my ears to sleep, but still, when he talks I pretend to listen to him, if only because it seems like the mature thing to do. When my father talks finance to my brother, Paul will cut him off, saying, "Fuck the stock talk, hoss, I ain't investing in shit." This rarely ends the economics lecture, but my brother wins bonus points for boldly voicing his uninterest, just as my father would do were someone to corner him and talk about Buddhism or the return of the clog. The two of them are unapologetically blunt. It's a quality my father admires so much, he's able to ignore the foul language completely. "That Paul," he says, "now *there's* a guy who knows how to communicate."

When words fail him, the Rooster has been known to communicate with his fists, which, though quick and solid, are no larger than a couple of tangerines. At five foot four, he's shorter than I am, stocky but not exactly intimidating. The year he turned thirty we celebrated Christmas at the home of my older sister Lisa. Paul arrived a few hours late with scraped palms and a black eye. There had been some encounter at a bar, but the details were sketchy.

"Some motherfucker told me to get the fuck out of his motherfucking face, so I said, 'Fuck off, fuckface.' "

"Then what?"

"Then he turned away and I reached up and punched him on the back of his motherfucking neck."

"What happened next?"

"What the fuck do you think happened next, bitch? I ran like hell and the motherfucker caught up with me in the fucking parking lot. He was all beefy, all flexed up and shit. The motherfucker had a taste for blood and he just pummeled my ass."

"When did he stop?"

My brother tapped his fingertips against the tabletop for a few moments before saying, "I'm guessing he stopped when he was fucking finished."

The physical pain had passed, but it bothered Paul that his face was "all lopsided and shit for the fucking holidays." That said, he retreated to the bathroom with my sister Amy's makeup kit and returned to the table with *two* black eyes, the second drawn on with mascara. This seemed to please him, and he wore his matching bruises for the rest of the evening.

"Did you get a load of that fake black eye?" my father asked. "That guy ought to do makeup for the movies. I'm telling you, the kid's a real artist."

Unlike the rest of us, the Rooster has always enjoyed our father's support and encouragement. With the dream of college officially dead and buried, he sent my brother to technical school, hoping he might develop an interest in computers. Three weeks into the semester, Paul dropped out, and my father, convinced that his son's lawn-mowing skills bordered on genius, set him up in the landscaping business. "I've seen him in action, and what he does is establish a pattern and really tackle it!"

Eventually my brother fell into the floor-sanding business. It's hard work, but he enjoys the satisfaction that comes with a well-finished rec room. He thoughtfully called his company Silly P's Hardwood Floors, Silly P being the name he would have chosen were he a rap star. When my father suggested that the word *silly* might frighten away some of the upper-tier customers, Paul considered changing the name to Silly Fucking P's Hardwood Floors. The work puts him in contact with plumbers and carpenters from such towns as Bunn and Clayton, men who offer dating advice such as "If she's old enough to bleed, she's old enough to breed."

"Old enough to what?" my father asks. "Oh, Paul, those aren't the sort of people you need to be associating with. What are you doing with hayseeds like that? The goal is to better yourself. Meet some intellectuals. Read a book!"

After all these years our father has never understood that we, his children, tend to gravitate toward the very people he's spent his life warning us about. Most of us have left town, but my brother remains in Raleigh. He was there when our mother died and still, years later, continues to help our father grieve: "The past is gone, hoss. What you need now is some motherfucking pussy." While my sisters and I offer our sympathy long-distance, Paul is the one who arrives at our father's house on Thanksgiving day, offering to prepare traditional Greek dishes to the best of his ability. It is a fact that he once made a tray of spanakopita using Pam rather than melted butter. Still, though, at least he tries.

When a hurricane damaged my father's house, my brother rushed over with a gas grill, three coolers full of beer, and an enormous Fuck-It Bucket — a plastic pail filled with jawbreakers and bite-size candy bars. ("When shit brings you down, just say 'fuck it,' and eat yourself some motherfucking candy.") There was no electricity for close to a week. The yard was practically cleared of trees, and rain fell through the dozens of holes punched into the roof. It was a difficult time, but the two of them stuck it out, my brother placing his small, scarred hand on my father's shoulder to say, "Bitch, I'm here to tell you that it's going to be all right. We'll get through this shit, motherfucker, just you wait."

The Youth in Asia

In the early 1960s, during what my mother referred to as "the tail end of the Lassie years," my parents were given two collies, which they named Rastus and Duchess. We were living in New York State, out in the country, and the dogs were free to race through the forest. They napped in meadows and stood knee-deep in frigid streams, co-stars in their own private dog-food commercial. According to our father, anyone could tell that the two of them were in love.

Late one evening, while lying on a blanket in the garage, Duchess gave birth to a litter of slick, potato-size puppies. When it looked as though one of them had died, our mother arranged the puppy in a casserole dish and popped it in the oven, like the witch in "Hansel and Gretel".

"Oh, keep your shirts on," she said. "It's only set on two

hundred. I'm not *baking* anyone, this is just to keep him warm."

The heat revived the sick puppy and left us believing that our mother was capable of resurrecting the dead.

Faced with the responsibilities of fatherhood, Rastus took off. The puppies were given away and we moved south, where the heat and humidity worked against a collie's best interests. Duchess's once beautiful coat now hung in ragged patches. Age set in and she limped about the house, clearing rooms with her suffocating farts. When finally, full of worms, she collapsed in the ravine beside our house, we reevaluated our mother's healing powers. The entire animal kingdom was beyond her scope; apparently she could resurrect only the cute dead.

The oven trick was performed on half a dozen peakish hamsters but failed to work on my first guinea pig, who died after eating a couple of cigarettes and an entire pack of matches.

"Don't take it too hard," my mother said, removing her oven mitts. "The world is full of guinea pigs: you can get another one tomorrow."

Eulogies tended to be brief, our motto being Another day, another collar.

A short time after Duchess died, our father came home with a German shepherd puppy. For reasons that were never fully explained, the privilege of naming the dog went to a friend of my older sister's, a fourteen-year-old girl named Cindy. She was studying German at the time, and after carefully examining the puppy and weighing it in her hands, she announced that it would be called Mädchen, which apparently meant "girl" to the Volks back in the Vaterland. We weren't wild about the name but considered ourselves lucky that Cindy wasn't studying one of the hard-to-pronounce Asian languages.

When she was six months old, Mädchen was hit by a car and killed. Her food was still in the bowl when our father brought home an identical German shepherd, which the same Cindy thoughtfully christened Mädchen II. This tag-team progression was disconcerting, especially to the new dog, which was expected to possess both the knowledge and the personality of her predecessor.

"Mädchen One would never have wet the floor like that," my father would scold, and the dog would sigh, knowing she was the canine equivalent of a rebound.

Mädchen Two never accompanied us to the beach and rarely posed in any of the family photographs. Once her puppyhood was spent, we lost all interest. "We ought to get a dog," we'd sometimes say, completely forgetting that we already had one. She came inside to eat, but most of her time was spent outside in the pen, slumped in the A-frame doghouse our father had designed and crafted from scrap pieces of redwood.

"Hey," he'd ask, "how many dogs can say they live in a redwood house?"

This always led to my mother's exhausted "Oh, Lou, how many dogs can say that they *don't* live in a goddamn redwood house?"

Throughout the collie and shepherd years we kept a succession of drowsy, secretive cats that seemed to enjoy a unique bond with our mother. "It's because I open their cans," she'd say, though we all knew it ran deeper than that. What they really had in common was their claws. That and a primal urge to destroy my father's golf bags. The first cat ran away, and the second one was hit by a car. The third passed into a disagreeable old age and died hissing at the kitten that had prematurely arrived to replace her. When, at the age of seven, the fourth cat was diagnosed with feline leukemia, my mother was devastated.

"I'm going to have Sadie put to sleep," she said. "It's for her own good, and I don't want to hear a word about it from any of you. This is hard enough as it is."

The cat was put down, and then came a series of crank phone calls and anonymous postcards orchestrated by my sisters and me. The cards announced a miraculous new cure for feline leukemia, and the callers identified themselves as representatives from *Cat Fancy* magazine. "We'd like to use Sadie as our September cover story and were hoping to schedule a photo shoot as soon as possible. Do you think you could have her ready by tomorrow?"

We thought a kitten might lift our mother's spirits, but she declined all offers. "That's it," she said. "My cat days are over."

When Mädchen Two developed splenic tumors, my father dropped everything and ran to her side. Evenings were spent at the animal hospital, lying on a mat outside of her cage and adjusting her IV. He'd never afforded her much attention when she was healthy, but her impending death awoke in him a great sense of duty. He was holding her paw when she died, and he spent the next several weeks asking us how many dogs could say they'd lived in a redwood house.

Our mother, in turn, frequently paused beside my father's tattered, urine-stained golf bag and relived memories of her own.

After spending a petless year with only one child still living at home, my parents visited a breeder and returned with a Great Dane they named Melina. They loved this dog in proportion to its size, and soon their hearts had no room for anyone else. In terms of mutual respect and admiration, their six children had been nothing more than a failed experiment. Melina was the real thing. The house was given over to the dog, rooms redecorated to suit her fancy. Enter your former bedroom and you'd be told, "You'd better not let Melina catch you in here," or, "This is where we come to peepee when there's nobody home to let us outside, right, girl!" The knobs on our dressers were whittled down to damp stumps, and our beds were matted with fine, short hairs. Scream at the mangled leather carcass lying at the foot of the stairs, and my parents would roar with laughter. "That's what you get for leaving your wallet on the kitchen table."

The dog was their first genuine common interest, and they loved it equally, each in his or her own way. Our mother's love tended toward the horizontal, a pet being little more than a napping companion, something she could look at and say, "That seems like a good idea. Scoot over, why don't you." A stranger peeking through the window might think that the two of them had entered a suicide pact. She and the dog sprawled like corpses, their limbs arranged in an eternal embrace. "God, that felt good," my mom would say, the two of them waking for a brief scratch. "Now let's go try it on the living-room floor."

My father loved the Great Dane for its size, and frequently took her on long, aimless drives, during which she'd stick her heavy, anvil-sized head out the window and leak great quantities of foamy saliva. Other drivers pointed and stared, rolling down their windows to shout, "Hey, you got a saddle for that thing?" When out for a walk there was the inevitable "Are you walking her, or is it the other way 'round?"

"Ha-ha!" our father always laughed, as if it were the first time he'd heard it. The attention was addictive, and he enjoyed a pride of accomplishment he never felt with any of us. It was as if he were somehow responsible for her beauty and stature, as if he'd personally designed her spots and trained her to grow to the size of a pony. When out with the dog, he carried a leash in one hand and a shovel in the other. "Just in case," he said.

"Just in case, what, she dies of a heart attack and you need to bury her?" I didn't get it.

"No," he said, "the shovel is for, you know, her . . . business."

My father was retired, but the dog had business.

I was living in Chicago when they first got Melina, and every time I came home the animal was bigger. Every time, there were more Marmaduke cartoons displayed on the refrigerator, and every time, my voice grew louder as I asked, "Who *are* you people?"

"Down, girl," my parents would chuckle as the dog jumped up, panting for my attention. Her great padded paws reached my waist, then my chest and shoulders, until eventually, her arms wrapped around my neck and, her head towering above my own, she came to resemble a dance partner scouting the room for a better offer.

"That's just her way of saying hello," my mother would chirp, handing me a towel to wipe off the dog's bubbling seepage. "Here, you missed a spot on the back of your head."

Among us children, Melina's diploma from obedience school was seen as the biggest joke since our brother's graduation from Sanderson High.

"So she's not book-smart," our mother said. "Big deal. I can fetch my own goddamn newspaper."

The dog's growth was monitored on a daily basis and every small accomplishment was captured on film. One could find few pictures of my sister Tiffany, but Melina had entire albums devoted to her terrible twos.

"Hit me," my mother said on one of my return visits home from Chicago. "No, wait, let me go get my camera." She left the room and returned a few moments later. "Okay, now you can hit me. Better yet, why don't you just *pretend* to hit me."

I raised my hand, and my mother cried out in pain. "Ow!" she yelled. "Somebody help me. This stranger is trying to hurt me and I don't know why."

I caught an advancing blur moving in from the left, and the next thing I knew I was down on the ground, the dog ripping significant holes in the neck of my sweater.

The camera flashed and my mother screamed with delight. "God, I love that trick."

I rolled over to protect my face. "It's not a trick."

My mother snapped another picture. "Oh, don't be so critical. It's close enough."

With us grown and out of the house, my sisters and I reasonably expected our parents' lives to stand still. Their assignment was to stagnate and live in the past. We were supposed to be the center of their lives, but instead, they had constructed a new family consisting of Melina and the founding members of her fan club. Someone who obviously didn't know her too well had given my mother a cheerful stuffed bear with a calico heart stitched to its chest. According to the manufacturer, the bear's name was Mumbles, and all it needed in order to thrive were two double-A batteries and a regular diet of hugs.

"Where's Mumbles?" my mother would ask, and the dog

would jump up and snatch the bear from its hiding place on top of the refrigerator, yanking its body this way and that in hopes of breaking its neck. Occasionally her teeth would press against the on switch, and the doomed thing would flail its arms, whispering one of its five recorded messages of goodwill.

"That's my girl," my mother would say. "We don't like Mumbles, do we?"

"We?"

During the final years of Mädchen Two and the first half of the Melina administration, I lived with a female cat named Neil. Dull gray in color, she'd been abandoned by a spooky alcoholic with long fingernails and a large collection of kimonos. He was a hateful man, and after he moved, the cat was taken in and renamed by my sister Gretchen, who later passed the animal on to me. My mother looked after Neil when I moved from Raleigh, and flew her to Chicago once I'd found a place and settled in. I'd taken the cheapest apartment I could find, and it showed. Though they were nice, my immigrant neighbors could see no connection between their personal habits and the armies of mice and roaches aggressively occupying the building. Welcoming the little change of scenery, entire families would regularly snack and picnic in the hallways, leaving behind candied fruits and half-eaten tacos. Neil caught fourteen mice, and scores of others escaped with missing limbs and tails. In Raleigh she'd just lain around the house doing nothing, but now she had a real job.

Her interests broadened and she listened intently to the

radio, captivated by the political and financial stories, which failed to engage me. "One more word about the Iran-Contra hearings, and you'll be sleeping next door with the aliens," I'd say, though we both knew that I didn't really mean it.

Neil was old when she moved to Chicago, and then she got older. The Oliver North testimony now behind her, she started leaving teeth in her bowl and developed the sort of breath that could remove paint. She stopped cleaning herself, and I took to bathing her in the sink. When she was soaking wet, I could see just how thin and brittle she really was. Her kidneys shrank to the size of raisins, and although I wanted what was best for her, I naturally assumed the vet was joking when he suggested dialysis. In addition to being elderly, toothless, and incontinent, it seemed that, for the cost of a few thousand dollars, she could also spend three days a week hooked up to a machine. "Sounds awfully tempting," I said. "Just give us a few days to think it over." I took her for a second opinion. Vet number two tested her blood and phoned me a few days later suggesting I consider euthanasia.

I hadn't heard that word since childhood and immediately recalled a mismatched pair of Japanese schoolboys standing alone in a deserted school yard. One of the boys, grossly obese, was attempting to climb a flagpole that towered high above him. Silhouetted against the darkening sky, he hoisted himself a few feet off the ground and clung there, trembling and out of breath. "I can't do it," he said. "This is too hard for me."

His friend, a gaunt and serious boy named Komatsu,

stood below him, offering encouragement. "Oh, but you *can* do it. You must," he said. "It is required."

This was a scene I had long forgotten, and thinking of it made me unbearably sad. The boys were characters from *Fatty and Skinny*, a Japanese movie regularly presented on *The CBS Children's Film Festival*, a weekly TV series hosted by two puppets and a very patient woman who pretended to laugh at their jokes. My sisters and I had watched the program every Saturday afternoon, our gasbag of a collie imposing frequent intermissions.

Having shimmied a few more inches up the flagpole, Fatty lost his grip and fell down into the sand. As he brushed himself off, Skinny ran down the mountain toward the fragile, papery house he shared with his family. This had been Fatty's last chance to prove himself. He'd thought his friend's patience was unlimited, but now he knew he was wrong. "Komatsuuuuuuuuuu!" he yelled. "Komatsu, please give me one more chance."

The doctor's voice called me back from the Japanese playground. "So the euthanasia," he said. "Are you giving it some thought?"

"Yes," I said. "As a matter of fact, I am."

In the end I returned to the animal hospital and had her put to sleep. When the vet injected the sodium pentobarbital, Neil fluttered her eyes, assumed a nap position, and died. My then boyfriend stayed to make arrangements, and I ran outside to blubber beside the parked and, unfortunately, locked car. Neil had gotten into her cat carrier believing she would eventually return to our apartment, and that tore me up. Someone had finally been naive enough to trust me, and I'd rewarded her with death. Racked by guilt, the youth in Asia sat at their desks and wept bitter tears.

A week after putting her to sleep, I received Neil's ashes in a forest green can. She'd never expressed any great interest in the outdoors, so I scattered her remains on the carpet and then vacuumed her back up. The cat's death struck me as the end of an era. It was, of course, the end of *her* era, but with the death of a pet there's always that urge to string black crepe over an entire ten- or twenty-year period. The end of my safe college life, the last of my thirty-inch waist, my faltering relationship with my first real boyfriend: I cried for it all and wondered why so few songs were written about cats.

My mother sent a consoling letter along with a check to cover the cost of the cremation. In the left-hand corner, on the line marked MEMO, she'd written, "Pet Burning." I had it coming.

When my mother died and was cremated herself, we worried that, acting on instinct, our father might run out and immediately replace her. Returning from the funeral, my brother, sisters, and I half expected to find some vaguely familiar Sharon Two standing at the kitchen counter and working the puzzle in *TV Guide.* "Sharon One would have gotten five across," our father would have scolded. "Come on, baby, get with it."

With my mother gone, my father and Melina had each other all to themselves. Though she now occupied the side of the bed left vacant by her former mistress, the dog knew she could never pass as a viable replacement. Her love was too fierce and simple, and she had no talent for argument. Yet she and my father honored their pledge to adore and protect each other. They celebrated anniversaries, regularly renewed their vows, and growled when challenged by outside forces.

"You want me to go *where?*" When invited to visit one of his children, my father would beg off, saying, "But I can't leave town. Who'd take care of Melina?" Mention a kennel, and he'd laugh. "You've got to be out of your mind. A kennel, ha! Hey, did you hear that, Melina? They want me to put you in prison."

Due to their size, Great Danes generally don't live very long. There are cheeses with a longer shelf life. At the age of twelve, gray bearded and teetering, Melina was a wonder of science. My father massaged her arthritic legs, carried her up the stairs, and lifted her in and out of bed. He treated her the way that men in movies treat their ailing wives, the way he might have treated my mother had she allowed such naked displays of helplessness and affection. Melina's era spanned the final dozen years of his married life. The dog had ridden in the family's last station wagon, attended my father's retirement party, and celebrated the elections of two Republican presidents. She grew weaker and lost her appetite, but against all advice, my father simply could not bear to let her go.

The youth in Asia begged him to end her life.

"I can't," he said. "This is too hard for me."

"Oh, but you must do it," said Komatsu. "It is required."

A month after Melina was put to sleep, my father returned to the breeder and came home with another Great Dane. A female like Melina, gray spots like Melina, only this one is named Sophie. He tries to love her but readily admits that he may have made a mistake. She's a nice enough dog, but the timing is off.

When walking Sophie through the neighborhood, my father feels not unlike the newly married senior stumbling behind his capricous young bride. The puppy's stamina embarrasses him, as does her blatant interest in young men. Passing drivers slow to a stop and roll down their windows. "Hey," they yell, "are you walking her, or is it the other way 'round?" Their words remind him of a more gracious era, of gentler forces straining against the well-worn leash. He still gets the attention, but now, in response, he just lifts his shovel and continues on his way.

The Learning Curve

A YEAR AFTER MY GRADUATION from the School of the Art Institute of Chicago, a terrible mistake was made and I was offered a position teaching a writing workshop. I had never gone to graduate school, and although several of my stories had been Xeroxed and stapled, none of them had ever been published in the traditional sense of the word.

Like branding steers or embalming the dead, teaching was a profession I had never seriously considered. I was clearly unqualified, yet I accepted the job without hesitation, as it would allow me to wear a tie and go by the name of Mr. Sedaris. My father went by the same name, and though he lived a thousand miles away, I liked to imagine someone getting the two of us confused. "Wait a minute," this someone might say, "are you talking about Mr. Sedaris the retired man living in North Carolina, or Mr. Sedaris the distinguished academic?"

The position was offered at the last minute, when the scheduled professor found a better-paying job delivering pizza. I was given two weeks to prepare, a period I spent searching for a briefcase and standing before my full-length mirror, repeating the words "Hello, class, my name is Mr. Sedaris." Sometimes I'd give myself an aggressive voice and firm, athletic timbre. This was the masculine Mr. Sedaris, who wrote knowingly of flesh wounds and tractor pulls. Then there was the ragged bark of the newspaper editor, a tone that coupled wisdom with an unlimited capacity for cruelty. I tried sounding businesslike and world-weary, but when the day eventually came, my nerves kicked in and the true Mr. Sedaris revealed himself. In a voice reflecting doubt, fear, and an unmistakable desire to be loved, I sounded not like a thoughtful college professor but, rather, like a high-strung twelve-year-old girl; someone named Brittany.

My first semester I had only nine students. Hoping they might view me as professional and well prepared, I arrived bearing name tags fashioned in the shape of maple leaves. I'd cut them myself out of orange construction paper and handed them out along with a box of straight pins. My fourth-grade teacher had done the same thing, explaining that we were to take only one pin per person. This being college rather than elementary school, I encouraged my students to take as many pins as they liked. They wrote their names upon their leaves, fastened them to their breast pockets, and bellied up to the long oak table that served as our communal desk.

"All right then," I said. "Okay, here we go." I opened my briefcase and realized that I'd never thought beyond this moment. The orange leaves were the extent of my lesson plan, but still I searched the empty briefcase, mindful that I had stupidly armed my audience with straight pins. I guess I'd been thinking that, without provocation, my students would talk, offering their thoughts and opinions on the issues of the day. I'd imagined myself sitting on the edge of the desk, overlooking a forest of raised hands. The students would simultaneously shout to be heard, and I'd pound on something in order to silence them. "Whoa people," I'd yell. "Calm down, you'll all get your turn. One at a time, one at a time."

The error of my thinking yawned before me. A terrible silence overtook the room, and seeing no other option, I instructed my students to pull out their notebooks and write a brief essay related to the theme of profound disappointment.

I'd always hated it when a teacher forced us to invent something on the spot. Aside from the obvious pressure, it seemed that everyone had his or her own little way of doing things, especially when it came to writing. Maybe someone needed a particular kind of lamp or pen or typewriter. In my experience, it was hard to write without your preferred tools, but impossible to write without a cigarette.

I made a note to bring in some ashtrays and then I rooted through the wastepaper basket for a few empty cans. Standing beneath the prominently displayed NO SMOKING sign, I distributed the cans and cast my cigarettes upon the table, encouraging my students to go at it. This, to me, was the very essence of teaching, and I thought I'd made a real breakthrough until the class asthmatic raised his hand, saying that, to the best of his knowledge, Aristophanes had never smoked a cigarette in his life. "Neither did Jane Austen," he said. "Or the Brontës."

I jotted these names into my notebook alongside the word *Troublemaker*, and said I'd look into it. Because I was the writing teacher, it was automatically assumed that I had read every leather-bound volume in the Library of Classics. The truth was that I had read none of those books, nor did I intend to. I bluffed my way through most challenges with dim memories of the movie or miniseries based upon the book in question, but it was an exhausting exercise and eventually I learned it was easier to simply reply with a question, saying, "I know what Flaubert means to *me*, but what do *you* think of her?"

As Mr. Sedaris I lived in constant fear. There was the perfectly understandable fear of being exposed as a fraud, and then there was the deeper fear that my students might hate me. I imagined them calling their friends on the phone. "Guess who *I* got stuck with," they'd say. Most dull teachers at least had a few credentials to back them up. They had a philosophy and a lesson plan and didn't need to hide behind a clip-on tie and an empty briefcase.

Whenever I felt in danger of losing my authority, I would cross the room and either open or close the door. A student needed to ask permission before regulating the temperature or noise level, but I could do so whenever I liked. It was the only activity sure to remind me that I was in charge, and I took full advantage of it.

"There he goes again," my students would whisper. "What's up with him and that door?"

The asthmatic transferred to another class, leaving me with only eight students. Of these, four were seasoned smokers who took long, contemplative drags and occasionally demonstrated their proficiency by blowing ghostly concentric rings that hovered like halos above their bowed heads. The others tried as best they could, but it wasn't pretty. By the end of the second session, my students had produced nothing but ashes. Their hacking coughs and complete lack of output suggested that, for certain writers, smoking was obviously not enough.

Thinking that a clever assignment might help loosen them up, I instructed my students to write a letter to their mothers in prison. They were free to determine both the crime and the sentence, and references to cellmates were strongly encouraged.

The group set to work with genuine purpose and enthusiasm, and I felt proud of myself, until the quietest member of the class handed in her paper, whispering that both her father and her uncle were currently serving time on federal racketeering charges.

"I just never thought of my mom going off as well," she said. "This was just a really . . . depressing assignment."

I'd never known what an actual child-to-parent prison letter might be like, but now I had a pretty clear idea. I envisioned two convicts sharing a cell. One man stood at the sink while the other lay on a bunk, reading his mail.

"Anything interesting?" the standing man asked.

"Oh, it's from my daughter," the other man said. "She's just started college, and apparently her writing teacher is a real asshole."

That was the last time I asked my students to write in class. From that point on all their stories were to be written at home on the subject of their choice. If I'd had my way, we would have all stayed home and conducted the class through smoke signals. As it was, I had to find some way to pass the time and trick my students into believing that they were getting an education. The class met twice a week for two hours a day. Filling an entire session with one activity was out of the question, so I began breaking each session into a series of brief, regularly scheduled discussion periods. We began each day with Celebrity Corner. This was an opportunity for the students to share interesting bits of information provided by friends in New York or Los Angeles who were forever claiming firsthand knowledge of a rock band's impending breakup or movie star's dark sexual secret. Luckily everyone seemed to have such a friend, and we were never short of material.

Celebrity Corner was followed by the Feedbag Forum, my shameless call for easy, one-pot dinner recipes, the type favored by elderly aunts and grandmothers whose dental status demanded that all meat fall from the bone without provocation. When asked what Boiled Beef Arkansas had to do with the craft of writing, I did not mention my recent purchase of a Crock-Pot; rather, I lied through my rotten teeth, explaining that it wasn't the recipe itself but the pacing that was of interest to the writer.

After the Feedbag Forum it was time for Pillow Talk, which was defined as "an opportunity for you to discuss your private sex lives in a safe, intellectual environment." The majority of my students were reluctant to share their experiences, so arrangements were made with the audiovisual department. I then took to wheeling in a big color television so that we might spend an hour watching *One Life to Live*. This was back when Victoria Buchanan passed out at her twentieth high-school reunion and came to remembering that rather than graduating with the rest of her class, she had instead hitchhiked to New York City, where she'd coupled with a hippie and given birth to a long-lost daughter. It sounds far-fetched, but like a roast forsaken in the oven or a rescheduled dental appointment, childbirth is one of those minor details that tends to slip the minds of most soap opera characters. It's a personality trait you've just got to accept.

On *General Hospital* or *Guiding Light* a similar story might come off as trite or even laughable. This, though, was *One Life to Live*, and no one could suddenly recall the birth of a child quite like Erika Slezak, who played both Victoria Buchanan and her alternate personality, Nicole Smith. I'd been in the habit of taping the show and watching it every night while eating dinner. Now that I was an academic, I could watch it in class and use the dinner hour to catch up on *All My Children.* A few students grumbled, but again I assured them that this was all part of my master plan.

Word came from the front office that there had been some complaints regarding my use of class time. This meant I'd have to justify my daily screenings with a homework assignment. Now the students were to watch an episode and write what I referred to as a "guessay," a brief prediction of what might take place the following day.

"Remember that this is not Port Charles or Pine Valley," I said. "This is Llanview, Pennsylvania, and we're talking about the Buchanan family."

It actually wasn't a bad little assignment. While the dialogue occasionally falters, you have to admire daytime dramas for their remarkable attention to plot. Yes, there were always the predictable kidnappings and summer love triangles, but a good show could always surprise you with something as simple as the discovery of an underground city. I'd coached my students through half a dozen episodes, giving them background information and explaining that missing children do not just march through the door ten minutes after the critical delivery flashback. The inevitable reunion must unfold delicately and involve at least two-thirds of the cast.

I thought I'd effectively conveyed the seriousness of the assignment. I thought that in my own way I had actually taught them something, so I was angry when their papers included such predictions as "the long-lost daughter turns out to be a vampire" and "the next day Vicki chokes to death while eating a submarine sandwich." The vampire business smacked of *Dark Shadows* reruns, and I refused to take it seriously. But choking to death on a sandwich, that was an insult. Victoria was a Buchanan and would never duck into a sub shop, much less choke to death in a single episode. Especially on a Wednesday. Nobody dies on a Wednesday — hadn't these people learned anything?

In the past I had tried my hardest to be understanding, going so far as to allow the conjugation of nouns and the use of such questionable words as *whateverishly*. This though, was going too far. I'd taught the Buchanans' Llanview just as my colleagues had taught Joyce's Dublin or Faulkner's Mississippi, but that was over now. Obviously certain people didn't deserve to watch TV in the middle of the afternoon. If my students wanted to stare at the walls for two hours a day, then fine, from here on out we'd just stick to the basics.

I don't know who invented the template for the standard writing workshop, but whoever it was seems to have struck the perfect balance between sadism and masochism. Here is a system designed to eliminate pleasure for everyone involved. The idea is that a student turns in a story, which is then read and thoughtfully critiqued by everyone in the class. In my experience the process worked, in that the stories were occasionally submitted, Xeroxed, and distributed hand to hand. They were folded into purses and knapsacks, but here the system tended to break down. Come critique time, most students behaved as if the assignment had been to confine the stories in a dark, enclosed area and test their reaction to sensory deprivation. Even if the papers were read out loud in class, the discussions were usually brief, as the combination of good manners and complete lack of interest kept most workshop participants from expressing their honest opinions.

With a few notable exceptions, most of the stories were thinly veiled accounts of the author's life as he or she attempted to complete the assignment. Roommates were forever stepping out of showers, and waitresses appeared out of nowhere to deliver the onion rings and breakfast burritos that stained the pages of the manuscripts. The sloppiness occasionally bothered me, but I had no room to complain. This was an art school, and the writing workshop was commonly known as the easiest way to fulfill one's mandatory English credits. My students had been admitted because they could admirably paint or sculpt or videotape their bodies in exhausting detail, and wasn't that enough? They told funny, compelling stories about their lives, but committing the details to paper was, for them, a chore rather than an aspiration. The way I saw it, if my students were willing to pretend I was a teacher, the least I could do was return the favor and pretend that they were writers. Even if someone had used his real name and recounted, say, a recent appointment with an oral surgeon, I would accept the story as pure fiction, saying, "So tell us, Dean, how did you come up with this person?"

The student might mumble, pointing to the bloodied cotton wad packed against his swollen gum, and I'd ask, "When did you decide that your character should seek treatment for his impacted molar?" This line of questioning allowed the authors to feel creative and protected anyone who held an unpopular political opinion.

"Let me get this straight," one student said. "You're telling me that if I say something out loud, it's me saying it, but if I write the exact same thing on paper, it's somebody else, right?"

"Yes," I said. "And we're calling that fiction."

The student pulled out his notebook, wrote something down, and handed me a sheet of paper that read, "That's the stupidest fucking thing I ever heard in my life."

They were a smart group.

As Mr. Sedaris I made it a point to type up a poorly spelled evaluation of each submitted story. I'd usually begin with the high points and end, a page or two later, by dispensing such sage professional advice as "Punctuation never hurt anyone" or "Think verbs!" I tended to lose patience with some of the longer dream sequences, but for the most part we all got along, and the students either accepted or politely ignored my advice.

Trouble arose only when authors used their stories to vindicate themselves against a great hurt or perceived injustice. This was the case with a woman whom the admissions office would have labeled a "returning student," meaning that her social life did not revolve around the cafeteria. The

woman was a good fifteen years older than me and clearly
disapproved of my teaching methods. She never contributed
to Pillow Talk or the Feedbag Forum, and I had good reason
to suspect it was she who had complained about the *One Life
to Live* episodes. With the teenage freshmen, I stood a chance,
but there was nothing I could do to please someone who
regularly complained that she'd wasted enough time already.
The class was divided into two distinct groups, with her on
one side and everyone else on the other. I'd tried everything
except leg irons, but nothing could bring the two sides together. It was a real problem.

The returning student had recently come through a difficult divorce, and because her pain was significant, she
wrongly insisted that her writing was significant as well. Titled
something along the lines of "I Deserve Another Chance," her
story was not well received by the class. Following the brief
group discussion, I handed her my written evaluation, which
she quietly skimmed over before raising her hand.

"Yes," she said. "If you don't mind, I have a little question."
She lit a cigarette and spent a moment identifying with the
smoldering match. "Who are *you*," she asked. "I mean, just
who in the hell are you to tell *me* that *my* story has no ending?"

It was a worthwhile question that was bound to be raised
sooner or later. I'd noticed that her story had ended in mid-
sentence, but that aside, who was I to offer criticism to anyone, especially in regard to writing? I'd meant to give the
issue some serious thought, but there had been shirts to iron

and name tags to make and, between one thing and another, I managed to put it out of my mind.

The woman repeated the question, her voice breaking. "Just who . . . in the stinking hell do you think . . . you are?"

"Can I give you an answer tomorrow?" I asked.

"No," she barked. "I want to know now. Who do you think you are?"

Judging from their expressions, I could see that the other side of the class was entertaining the same question. Doubt was spreading through the room like the cold germs seen in one of those slow-motion close-ups of a sneeze. I envisioned myself burning on a pyre of dream sequences, and then the answer came to me.

"Who am I?" I asked. "I am the only one who is paid to be in this room." This was nothing I'd necessarily want to embroider on a pillow, but still, once the answer left my mouth, I embraced it as a perfectly acceptable teaching philosophy. My previous doubts and fears evaporated, as now I knew that I could excuse anything. The new Mr. Sedaris would never again back down or apologize. From here on out, I'd order my *students* to open and close the door and let *that* remind me that I was in charge. We could do whatever I wanted because I was a certified professional — it practically said so right there on my paycheck. My voice deepened as I stood to straighten my tie. "All right then," I said. "Does anyone else have a stupid question for Mr. Sedaris?"

The returning student once again raised her hand. "It's

a personal question, I know, but exactly how much is the school paying you to be in this room?"

I answered honestly, and then, for the first time since the beginning of the school year, my students came together as one. I can't recall which side started it, I remember only that the laughter was so loud, so violent and prolonged that Mr. Sedaris had to run and close the door so that the real teachers could conduct their business in peace.

Big Boy

It was Easter Sunday in Chicago, and my sister Amy and I were attending an afternoon dinner at the home of our friend John. The weather was nice, and he'd set up a table in the backyard so that we might sit in the sun. Everyone had taken their places, when I excused myself to visit the bathroom, and there, in the toilet, was the absolute biggest turd I have ever seen in my life — no toilet paper or anything, just this long and coiled specimen, as thick as a burrito.

I flushed the toilet, and the big turd trembled. It shifted position, but that was it. This thing wasn't going *anywhere*. I thought briefly of leaving it behind for someone else to take care of, but it was too late for that. Too late because, before getting up from the table, I'd stupidly told everyone where I was going. "I'll be back in a minute," I'd said. "I'm just going to run to the bathroom." My whereabouts were public knowledge. I should have said I was going to make a phone call. I'd planned to urinate and maybe run a little water over my face, but now I had this to deal with.

The tank refilled, and I made a silent promise. The deal was that if this thing would go away, I'd repay the world by performing some unexpected act of kindness. I flushed the toilet a second time, and the big turd spun a lazy circle. "Go on," I whispered. "Scoot! Shoo!" I turned away, ready to perform my good deed, but when I looked back down, there it was, bobbing to the surface in a fresh pool of water.

Just then someone knocked on the door, and I started to panic.

"Just a minute."

At an early age my mother sat me down and explained that everyone has bowel movements. "Everyone," she'd said. "Even the president and his wife." She'd mentioned our neighbors, the priest, and several of the actors we saw each week on television. I'd gotten the overall picture, but natural or not, there was no way I was going to take responsibility for this one.

"Just a minute."

I seriously considered lifting this turd out of the toilet and tossing it out the window. It honestly crossed my mind, but John lived on the ground floor and a dozen people were seated at a picnic table ten feet away. They'd see the window open and notice something dropping to the ground. And these were people who would surely gather round and investigate. Then there I'd be with my unspeakably filthy hands, trying to explain that *it wasn't mine.* But why bother throwing it out the window if it wasn't mine? No one would have believed me except the person who had left it in the first place, and chances were pretty slim that the freak in question would suddenly step forward and own up to it. I was trapped.

"I'll be out in a second!"

I scrambled for a plunger and used the handle to break the turd into manageable pieces, all the while thinking that it *wasn't fair,* that this was technically *not my job.* Another flush and it still didn't go down. *Come on, pal. Let's move it.* While waiting for the tank to refill, I thought maybe I should wash my hair. It wasn't dirty, but I needed some excuse to cover the amount of time I was spending in the bathroom. *Quick,* I thought. *Do something.* By now the other guests were probably thinking I was the type of person who uses dinner parties as an opportunity to defecate and catch up on my reading.

"Here I come. I'm just washing up."

One more flush and it was all over. The thing was gone and out of my life. I opened the door to find my friend Janet, who said, "Well, it's about time." And I was left thinking that the person who'd abandoned the huge turd had no problem with it, so why did I? Why the big deal? Had it been left there to teach me a lesson? Had a lesson been learned? Did it have anything to do with Easter? I resolved to put it all behind me, and then I stepped outside to begin examining the suspects.

The Great Leap Forward

WHEN I FIRST MOVED TO NEW YORK, I shared a reasonably priced two-bedroom apartment half a block from the Hudson River. I had no job at the time and was living off the cruel joke I referred to as my savings. In the evenings, lacking anything better to do, I used to head east and stare into the windows of the handsome, single-family town houses, wondering what went on in those well-appointed rooms. What would it be like to have not only your own apartment but an entire building in which you could do whatever you wanted? I'd watch a white-haired man slipping out of his back brace and ask myself what he'd done to deserve such a privileged life. Had I been able to swap places with him, I would have done so immediately.

I'd never devoted much time to envy while living in

Chicago, but there it had been possible to rent a good-size apartment and still have enough money left over for a movie or a decent cut of meat. To be broke in New York was to feel a constant, needling sense of failure, as you were regularly confronted by people who had not only more but much, much more. My daily budget was a quickly spent twelve dollars, and every extravagance called for a corresponding sacrifice. If I bought a hot dog on the street, I'd have to make up that money by eating eggs for dinner or walking fifty blocks to the library rather than taking the subway. The newspaper was fished out of trash cans, section by section, and I was always on the lookout for a good chicken-back recipe. Across town, over in the East Village, the graffiti was calling for the rich to be eaten, imprisoned, or taxed out of existence. Though it sometimes seemed like a nice idea, I hoped the revolution would not take place during my lifetime. I didn't want the rich to go away until I could at least briefly join their ranks. The money was tempting. I just didn't know how to get it.

I was nearing the end of a brief seasonal job when I noticed that my favorite town house had been put up for sale. "A Federal Gem," the papers would have called it. Four stories tall, the building stood on a quiet, tree-lined block enclosing a private garden. As far as I was concerned, the house belonged to me. I'd spent a lot of time spying into the walnut-paneled second-floor study and imagining myself dusting the bookcases. It would take a lot of work to keep the place clean, but I was willing to make the sacrifice.

A few months after being put on the market, the building

was sold and painted hot pink with tangerine trim. The combination of colors gave the house a raw, jittery feeling. Stare at the facade for more than a minute, and the doors and windows appeared to tremble, as if suffering the effects of a powerful amphetamine.

Because I had always noticed this house, I found it remarkable when, through the recommendation of a casual acquaintance, the new owner hired me to work three days a week as her personal assistant. Valencia was a striking, tightly wound Colombian woman with a closetful of short skirts and a singular talent for appalling her neighbors. After painting the walnut-paneled library a screeching canary yellow, she strung a clothesline across the nineteenth-century wrought-iron balcony the former owner had brought up from New Orleans.

"Show me where there is a law who says I cannot dry my clothes in sunshine," she said, crumpling up one of the several anonymous letters of complaint. "Maybe these people should just mind to their own business for one time in their life and leave me alone, my God."

It was rumored that Valencia was some sort of heiress and had paid for the million-dollar house in cash, much the same way a normal person might buy a belt or an electric skillet. Money seemed to embarrass her, and though she was obviously quite well off, she preferred to pretend otherwise. The house was furnished with broken tables and chairs she'd picked up off the street, and every service was haggled over. If a cabdriver charged her four dollars, she'd wrangle him down to three. Should someone demand the previously agreed-upon price, he or she was accused of trying to fleece a poor immigrant woman with a small, struggling business and a child to feed. Worn out by the bickering, a surprising number of people eventually caved in. Often these were cash-strapped independent merchants and laborers, and I was always surprised by the joy she took in saving a few dollars at their expense.

Valencia's business was a small publishing company she ran from her garishly painted fourth-floor study. It was more a hobby than a moneymaker, but the work satisfied her dual interests in art and in a certain, listlike style of writing. In her first year of operation she had produced two volumes of poetry, written by men known mainly for their violent tempers. Once or twice a week an order would come in, and it was my job to fill it. There were occasional errands to run or letters to Xerox, but for the most part all I did was sit at my desk and mentally redecorate the house. A go-getter might have dreamt up clever ways of promoting the two unpopular titles, but I have no mind for business and considered staying awake to be enough of an accomplishment.

Around the first of the month, when the bills came due for the phone, gas, and electricity, Valencia would have me go through the books and make a list of everyone who owed her money. She'd notice, for example, that a bookstore in London had an overdue account of seventeen dollars. "Seventeen dollars! I want you to call them now and tell them to send it to me."

I'd point out that the long-distance call would cost more than the money she was owed, but she didn't seem to care, saying that it was the principle that bothered her. "Call them now before they have their tea."

I'd then pick up the phone and pretend to dial. There was no way I could get heavy-handed and demand that an English person send me money, even if he owed it to me personally. Holding the receiver up to my mouth, I'd look out across the garden and into the orderly homes of Valencia's neighbors. Uniformed maids entered rooms carrying tea services on silver trays. Men and women sat on chairs with four legs and stared at their walls without the benefit of sunglasses. What worried me was the thought that I actually belonged in Valencia's house, that of all the homes in New York, my place was here with the Barefoot Contessa. "London's not answering," I'd say. "I think today is a British national holiday."

"Well, then, I think it would be good for you to call that store in Michigans who owe us the twelve dollars and fifty cents."

In the late afternoon we would often be visited by one or more of the failed Beat poets who always, very coincidentally, seemed to find themselves in the neighborhood. They were known for their famous friendships rather than the work they had produced, but that was enough for Valencia, who collected these men much the same way that her neighbors collected Regency tea caddies or Staffordshire hounds. Occasionally these poets would show up drunk, carrying found objects on to which they had scrawled cryptic messages. "Look what I did," they'd say. "Want to buy it?" Such works decorated the house, and I was often scolded for accidentally throwing away Robert's Styrofoam cup or Douglas's very special paint stick. Valencia was incredibly generous to these deadbeats. She memorized their poetry and excused their bad behavior. She poured them drinks and forced them to eat, but had she been as poor as she normally pretended to be, I doubt they would have wanted anything to do with her. In their presence she was charming and attentive, but they seemed to need more than just her friendship. Watching her in their company, I could understand why wealthy people usually had other wealthy people for friends. It was one thing to be disliked, but I imagine it must really smart to find yourself repeatedly taken advantage of.

My career as a personal assistant hit rock bottom one summer morning when Valencia greeted me with a flyer she'd taken from the window of an exotic-bird shop located on the corner. Beneath a fuzzy Xeroxed photo of what appeared to be a chicken was a description of a missing African grey parrot that had flown out of the store when a customer opened the door. It was noted that the bird answered to the name of Cheeky and that a $750 reward had been offered for its return.

"So there it is," Valencia said. "We will find this Cheeky bird, split the money, and then we will be rich!"

The chances of finding the parrot struck me as fairly slim. It had already enjoyed two days of freedom, and even on foot it would have easily made Brooklyn long ago. I went to work filling a book order, annoyed that Valencia took such great pleasure in pretending to be poor. Finding the bird would have been nice, sure, but it was silly to act as though she needed that money to survive. Somewhere along the way she'd got the idea that broke people led richer lives than everybody else, that they were nobler or more intelligent. In an effort to keep me noble, she was paying me less than she'd paid her previous assistant. Half my paychecks bounced, and she refused to reimburse me for my penalty charges, claiming that it was my bank's fault, not hers.

I was stuffing a book into an envelope when Valencia hissed, "Psst. David, look! Outside! I think I see the seven-hundred-and-fifty-dollar bird."

I looked through the open window, where, standing on the branch of a ginkgo tree, a male pigeon was examining his misshapen foot.

"Call him into the house," Valencia whispered. "Tell him you have some good bread for him to eat, and he will come."

I told her it was just a pigeon, but she denied it, holding up the smudgy Xerox as proof. "Call him by the name of Cheeky. Grab him with your hands, and we will split the money."

I thought once more of my bounced paychecks and realized that had this been the actual parrot, she would have found some way to renege on the deal and change the split from the promised fifty-fifty. I could clearly see her saying that she had been the first one to spot the bird and that she deserved more because it had been captured on her property.

In the past I had put up with her tantrums and said nothing when she'd yelled at me in front of the deadbeats, but this was asking too much. Although I could humor her by courting the bird, I knew that I definitely could not call him Cheeky. It was just too embarrassing.

"What are you waiting for?" she asked. "Hurry, before it's too late."

I lowered my voice and produced a series of gentle kissing noises. I promised food and comfort, but the pigeon had no interest in entering the house. He stared past me, as if judging the broken furniture and brightly painted walls, and then he flew away.

"How could you let him fly like that?" Valencia screamed. "We could have made important money, but instead, you were so stupid with those noises you preferred. Really, how could you!"

She threw herself on the bed she kept parked in the corner and sulked for a while before picking up the chipped telephone and calling someone in her native land. I'd studied Spanish in high school but had no idea whom she was calling or what they were talking about. Her tone of voice suggested that she was possibly begging someone for a heart or kidney, something urgent. The pleading was followed by an extended period of screaming that ultimately gave way to more begging. Such calls were common, and though she sometimes wept, she never mentioned the conversation after slamming down the receiver.

Valencia had been on the phone for maybe ten minutes

when the Spanish stopped and she switched to English. "David! He's back. It's the seven-hundred-and-fifty-dollar bird, and this time he wants to come into the house. Get him. Get Cheeky!"

It was another pigeon, this one with two healthy feet and a noticeably shorter attention span. He flew away, and again I was screamed at.

"You are competent at nothing. I cannot believe this situation I am having with you. What good is a person who cannot even catch a bird?"

The scene repeated itself through the course of the week and marked the beginning of the end for Valencia and me. She started calling early on my scheduled days, saying that she wouldn't be needing any help. I knew that she had recently bought a computer and was paying a college student to teach her how to use it. The student was cheerful and efficient and enjoyed Beat poetry. If asked to, she could have capably wrangled seventeen dollars from the English or caught a pigeon with her bare hands. The name *Cheeky* would have come easily to her, so it made sense to phase me out. I should have handed in my resignation, but as lousy and low-paying as the job was, I didn't want to have to look for another one. And so I stayed and waited to be fired.

I was down to a day and a half a week when Valencia called a mover to cart a load of furniture to an apartment she'd rented for one of the deadbeats. The man came alone, not bringing any helpers, as he'd been told it was a one-person job. It's hard for one person to carry a sofa down three flights of stairs, so, seeing as I had nothing better to do, I offered to help. The man's name was Patrick, and he spoke in a soft, hypnotic voice that made everything he said sound wise and comforting. "I can see that you've really got your hands full with that one," he said, rolling his eyes toward Valencia's office. "I've known broads like that all my life. She wants to be artsy and has settled on being cheap. I can tell I won't be getting a tip out of her."

After we'd carried the furniture to the deadbeat's new apartment, Patrick offered me a job, and I took it.

"Terrific," he said. "Get yourself a back brace, and I'll see you in the morning."

Because he was a card-carrying communist, Patrick hated being referred to as the boss. "This is a collective," he'd say. "Sure, I might happen to own the truck, but that doesn't make me any more valuable than the next guy. If I'm better than you, it's only because I'm Irish."

I'd never cared for any of the self-proclaimed Marxists I'd known back in college, but Patrick was different. One look at his teeth, and you could understand his crusade for universal health care. Both his glasses and his smile were held together with duct tape. Notable too was his willingness to engage in actual physical work. The communists I'd known in the past had always operated on the assumption that come the revolution, they'd be the ones lying around party headquarters with clipboards in their hands. They couldn't manage to wash a coffee mug, yet they'd been more than willing to criticize the detergent manufacturer.

Patrick's mugs were clean and neatly lined up on the drainboard. He lived alone in a tiny rent-controlled apartment filled with soft snack foods, letters from imprisoned radicals, and the sorts of newspapers that have no fashion section. His moving collective consisted of him, a dented bread truck, and a group of full- and part-time helpers hired according to availability and the size of any given job. Together we resembled the cast of a dopey situation comedy, something called *Grin and Bear It*, or *Hello, Dolly*. The part-time helpers included Lyle, a guitar-playing folksinger from Queens, and Ivan, a Russian immigrant on medication for what had been diagnosed as residual schizophrenia. I worked full-time, most often with a convicted murderer named Richie, who, at six feet four and close to 350 pounds, was a poster boy for both the moving industry and the failure of the criminal rehabilitation system. Convicted at the age of fifteen, he had served ten years in a combination of juvenile and adult penitentiaries on charges of arson and second-degree murder. The victim had been his sister's boyfriend, whom Richie had burned to death because, in his words, "I don't know. The guy was an asshole. What more do you want?" He thought of what he'd said and then retracted it, saying, "Rather, I found him to be untrustworthy. How's that?" In an effort to impress his latest parole officer, Richie was trying to improve his vocabulary. "I can't promise I'll never kill anyone again," he once said, strapping a refrigerator to his back. "It's unrealistic to live your life within such strict parameters."

It would be a stretch to say that I enjoyed coaxing mattresses up five flights of stairs, but it was nice to work as part of a team. The money was nothing compared with what other people earned answering phones or slipping suppositories into the rectums of senior citizens, but it was more than I had earned working for Valencia. The cash was bounceproof, and most everyone included a tip. After having spent a year and a half cooped up in a little office, it felt good to get out and move around. Rego Park, Bayside, Harlem, Coney Island, the job introduced me to the various neighborhoods of Manhattan and the surrounding boroughs. It gave me a chance to look into people's lives, to meet my fellow New Yorkers and carry their things.

Because Patrick didn't believe in having himself bonded, we rarely moved anything of great value, no museum-quality paintings or extraordinary pieces of furniture. Most of our customers were moving into places they couldn't quite afford. Their new, higher rents meant that they'd have to cut back on their spending, to work longer hours, or try to wean themselves off their costly psychiatrists. They were anxious about their future and quick to complain should a part of their past get scratched or broken. "The transitory state fucks with their heads," Richie explained during my first week of work. "Me, I just try to ignore their stressed-outedness and concentrate on the gratuity."

Moving heavy objects allowed me to feel manly in the eyes of other men. With the women it didn't matter, but I enjoyed subtly intimidating the guys with bad backs who thought they were helping out by telling us how to pack the truck. The thinking was that because we were furniture movers, we obviously weren't too bright. In addition to being strong and stupid, we were also thought of as dangerous. It might have been an old story to Patrick and the others, but I got a kick out of being mistaken as volatile. All I had to do was throw down my dolly with a little extra force, and a bossy customer would say, "Let's just all calm down and try to work this out."

I began to change in subtle ways and quickly lost patience with people who owned too many books. What had once seemed an honorable inclination now struck me as a heavy and inconvenient affectation. The conversation wasn't as sparkling, but I found that I much preferred the stuffed-animal collectors. Boxes of records made me think that LPs should be outlawed or at least limited to five per person, and I soon came to despise the type who packs even her empty shampoo bottles, figuring she'll sort things out and throw them away once she's settled into her new place.

When faced with an apartment full of boxes, I'd pretend to be an ant assigned to transport sandwich crumbs back to my colony. There was no use trying to estimate how many trips it might involve, as that sort of thinking only wore me out in advance. Instead, I just took it box by box until it was my turn to guard the truck. Once we reached the new building, the process would be repeated, hopefully with an elevator. Standing in their new apartments, the air noxious with the smell of paint, the customers would determine the order of their new lives. "The sofa bed goes here — no, over there maybe. What do you think?" The schizophrenic was the best at giving decorating advice, though Richie wasn't bad, either.

After a job was finished, we'd stand on the street drinking beer or foul-tasting Gatorade. The tip would be discussed, as would the disadvantages of living in this particular neighborhood. It was generally agreed that a coffin-size studio on Avenue D was preferable to living in one of the boroughs. Moving from one Brooklyn or Staten Island neighborhood to another was fine, but unless you had children to think about, even the homeless saw it as a step down to leave Manhattan. Customers quitting the island for Astoria or Cobble Hill would claim to welcome the change of pace, saying it would be nice to finally have a garden or live a little closer to the airport. They'd put a good face on it, but one could always detect an underlying sense of defeat. The apartments might be bigger and cheaper in other places, but one could never count on their old circle of friends making the long trip to attend a birthday party. Even Washington Heights was considered a stretch. People referred to it as Upstate New York, though it was right there in Manhattan.

Our bottles drained, Patrick would carry us back to what everyone but Lyle agreed was the center of the universe.

Moving people from one place to another made me feel as though I performed a valuable service, recognized and appreciated by the city at large. In the grand scheme of things, I finally had a role to play. My place was not with Valencia but here, riding in a bread truck with my friends. My friend the communist, my friend the schizophrenic, and my friend the murderer.

The first of the month was always the busiest time, but there were more than enough minor jobs and unhappy marriages to pull us through. In other parts of the country people tried to stay together for the sake of the children. In New York they tried to work things out for the sake of the apartment. Leaving a spacious, reasonably priced one-bedroom in the middle of the month usually signified that someone had done something really bad. We'd empty a place of half its possessions and listen to the details as we drove the former tenant to a quickly rented storage space. The truck made a good deal of noise, and although the injured party was always eager to talk, he had to significantly raise his voice to be heard. I liked being told these stories, but it was odd hearing such personal information shouted rather than whispered.

"THEN SHE WHAT?" Richie or I would scream.

"FUCKED HER EX-BOYFRIEND ON THIS SOFA I'D BOUGHT FOR OUR ANNIVERSARY."

"ON THE WHAT?"

"THE SOFA I'M SITTING ON. SHE FUCKED HER EX-BOYFRIEND ON THIS SOFA."

"HOW MANY TIMES?" we'd ask.

"HUH?"

"I SAID, 'HOW MANY TIMES?'"

"JUST ONCE THAT I KNOW OF, BUT ISN'T THAT ENOUGH?"

"IT DEPENDS. HOW MUCH WAS YOUR RENT?"

When the citizens of New York went looking for a new apartment, they came to us. Some movers charged for their inside information, but, with the exception of Richie, we gave it away for free. Strangers would often flag down the loaded van and ask where we were coming from. "Do you know if it's already been rented? Does it have a tub or a shower?" They asked the same thing of the emergency medical crews pulling up to the hospital morgue. "What floor did the victim live on? Did the apartment get much light?"

I'd been raised with the impression that it took a certain amount of know-how to get by in New York, but a surprising number of our customers proved me wrong. Here were people who packed two hundred pounds of dishes into a single box the size of a doghouse, or even worse, people who didn't pack at all. One evening we went to move an attractive young woman who found it charming to spell the name Kim with an *h*, a *y*, and two *m*s. The door opened to the sound of nerve-shattering club music broadcast from an enormous stereo system. Popcorn snapped away on the stovetop and everything appeared to be in its rightful place. I assumed that we had the wrong apartment and was ready to apologize when she said, "Are you the movers? Great, come on in."

The phone rang and she talked for a few moments before

covering the mouthpiece to say, "I couldn't find any boxes or anything, so just . . . you know."

"Just 'you know' what?" Richie asked. "Just use our fucking magic powers or just, you know, go home?"

He and I were ready to leave. It irritated us that this girl couldn't even manage to pack. You don't just place a red-hot skillet on the floor of a moving truck, and besides, if she couldn't bother to round up a few dozen boxes, there was little chance she'd come through with much of a tip. Khymm struck me as the sort of person who had always gotten by on her looks. People had probably forgiven her for all kinds of things, but I doubted she'd get much sympathy out of Patrick. It was my understanding that communists preferred beefy, corn-fed girls with thick ankles and strong backs, all the better for threshing wheat and lugging heavy sacks of rice.

"Well?" Richie asked.

Patrick threw up his hands. "Oh, what the hell. We're here, aren't we?"

The young woman had a small dog, a Pomeranian, that yapped nonstop during the three hours it took to empty the apartment. She herself did nothing to help but rather talked on the phone, occasionally pausing to yell, "That's very collectible," or "Be careful with the fish, I'm pretty sure the female is pregnant." While climbing the three flights of stairs for another armload of shampoo bottles, I entertained cruel fantasies, which grew more pronounced once we'd packed up the truck and arrived at her new apartment, on the fifth floor of yet another walk-up building. Just as I had predicted, our tip consisted of a toothy smile and the ridiculous suggestion that we have a nice evening. Patrick gave us a little something extra for our troubles but refused to join in when Richie and I grumbled about the girl's prizewinning idiocy.

"Oh, give her a break. She was a good kid." He could be very unpredictable that way. Sometimes we'd walk into an organized, well-packed apartment, and if the client was male and obviously very successful, Patrick would cancel the job, claiming that his axle had just broken or that the truck's transmission had given out. "Sorry, friend, but I just can't do it." He'd give the guy the number of one of his competitors and then he would leave, delighted by the great inconvenience he had caused.

"Guys like that are bad news," he'd say, heading back to the truck. "So how about it, boys, are any of you up for a piping hot cup of coffee? My treat."

I was rarely appeased by the words *piping hot*. I didn't want a cup of coffee, I wanted to work. "What was wrong with that guy?" I'd ask. "It was an elevator building, for God's sake. That was good money."

Patrick would throw back his head and let out his hearty communist laugh, an extended bray that suggested I was young and could not yet tell the difference between good money and bad.

"We'll do a big job tomorrow," he'd say. "Relax, brother. How much money do you need?"

"Enough for a town house," I'd say.

"You don't want a town house."

"Yes, I do."

"Well, then, you're definitely in the wrong business."

He was right about that. Carrying boxes up and down stairs wasn't going to earn me a million dollars. Still, the extra money in my pocket allowed me to walk down the street not caring that other people had more than I did. I'd go to a movie or buy a dime bag of pot from Richie and not feel burdened by envy. I just had to understand that for Patrick, moving a certain kind of person was the equivalent of me calling a pigeon Cheeky — it simply wasn't worth the money to him. Maybe he felt those men looking at his teeth and thinking him a loser. In their great, tenacious drive to succeed, perhaps Patrick saw the futility of his own struggle. Detailed questions about his decisions only led to the quoting of Marx and Lenin, so I soon learned to stop asking.

The best of times were snappy autumn afternoons when we'd finished moving a two-bedroom customer from Manhattan to some faraway neighborhood in Brooklyn or Queens. The side doors would be open as we crowded in the front seat, Patrick listening to a taped translation of Chairman Mao boasting about "the great leap forward." Traffic would be heavy on the bridge due to an accident, and because we were paid for travel time, we'd hope that the pileup involved at least one piece of heavy machinery. When the tape became too monotonous, I'd ask Richie about his days at the reformatory and pleasantly drowse as he spoke of twelve-year-old car thieves and boys who had killed their brothers over an ice-cream sandwich. Patrick would get involved, saying that violent crime was a natural consequence of the capitalist system, and then, eventually, the New York skyline would appear on the horizon and we'd all stop talking. If you happen to live there, it's always refreshing to view Manhattan from afar. Up close the city constitutes an oppressive series of staircases, but from a distance it inspires fantasies of wealth and power so profound that even our communists are temporarily rendered speechless.

Today's Special

It is his birthday, and Hugh and I are seated in a New York restaurant, awaiting the arrival of our fifteen-word entrées. He looks very nice, dressed in the suit and sweater that have always belonged to him. As for me, I own only my shoes, pants, shirt, and tie. My jacket belongs to the restaurant and was offered as a loan by the maître d', who apparently thought I would feel more comfortable dressed to lead a high-school marching band.

I'm worrying the thick gold braids decorating my sleeves when the waiter presents us with what he calls "a little something to amuse the palette." Roughly the size and color of a Band-Aid, the amusement floats on a shallow, muddy puddle of sauce and is topped with a sprig of greenery.

"And this would be . . . what, exactly?" Hugh asks.

"This," the waiter announces, "is our raw Atlantic sword-fish served in a dark chocolate gravy and garnished with fresh mint."

"Not again," I say. "Can't you guys come up with something a little less conventional?"

"Love your jacket," the waiter whispers.

As a rule, I'm no great fan of eating out in New York restaurants. It's hard to love a place that's outlawed smoking but finds it perfectly acceptable to serve raw fish in a bath of chocolate. There are no normal restaurants left, at least in our neighborhood. The diners have all been taken over by precious little bistros boasting a menu of indigenous American cuisine. They call these meals "traditional," yet they're rarely the American dishes I remember. The club sandwich has been pushed aside in favor of the herb-encrusted medallions of baby artichoke hearts, which never leave me thinking, Oh, right, those! I wonder if they're as good as the ones my mom used to make.

Part of the problem is that we live in the wrong part of town. SoHo is not a macaroni salad kind of place. This is where the world's brightest young talents come to braise caramelized racks of corn-fed songbirds or offer up their famous knuckle of flash-seared crappie served with a collar of chided ginger and cornered by a tribe of kiln-roasted Chilean toadstools, teased with a warm spray of clarified musk oil. Even when they promise something simple, they've got to tart it up — the meatloaf has been poached in sea water, or there are figs in the tuna salad. If cooking is an art, I think we're in our Dada phase.

I've never thought of myself as a particularly finicky eater, but it's hard to be a good sport when each dish seems to include no fewer than a dozen ingredients, one of which I'm bound to dislike. I'd order the steak with a medley of suffocated peaches, but I'm put off by the aspirin sauce. The sea scallops look good until I'm told they're served in a broth of malt liquor and mummified litchi nuts. What I really want is a cigarette, and I'm always searching the menu in the hope that some courageous young chef has finally recognized tobacco as a vegetable. Bake it, steam it, grill it, or stuff it into littleneck clams, I just need something familiar that I can hold on to.

When the waiter brings our entrées, I have no idea which plate might be mine. In yesterday's restaurants it was possible both to visualize and to recognize your meal. There were always subtle differences, but for the most part, a lamb chop tended to maintain its basic shape. That is to say that it looked choplike. It had a handle made of bone and a teardrop of meat hugged by a thin rind of fat. Apparently, though, that was too predictable. Order the modern lamb chop, and it's likely to look no different than your companion's order of shackled pompano. The current food is always arranged into a senseless, vertical tower. No longer content to recline, it now reaches for the sky, much like the high-rise buildings lining our city streets. It's as if the plates were valuable parcels of land and the chef had purchased one small lot and unlimited air rights. Hugh's saffron linguini resembles a miniature turban, topped with architectural spires of shrimp. It stands there in the center while the rest of the vast, empty plate looks though it's been leased out as a possible parking lot. I had ordered the steak, which, bowing to the same minimalist fashion, is served without the bone, the thin slices of beef stacked to resemble a funeral pyre. The potatoes I'd been expecting have apparently either been clarified to an essence or were used to stoke the grill.

"Maybe," Hugh says, "they're inside your tower of meat."

This is what we have been reduced to. Hugh blows the yucca pollen off his blackened shrimp while I push back the sleeves of my borrowed sport coat and search the meat tower for my promised potatoes.

"There they are, right there." Hugh uses his fork to point out what could easily be mistaken for five cavity-riddled molars. The dark spots must be my vegetable.

Because I am both a glutton and a masochist, my standard complaint, "That was so bad," is always followed by "And there was so little of it!"

Our plates are cleared, and we are presented with dessert menus. I learn that spiced ham is no longer considered just a luncheon meat and that even back issues of *Smithsonian* can be turned into sorbets.

"I just couldn't," I say to the waiter when he recommends the white chocolate and wild loganberry couscous.

"If we're counting calories, I could have the chef serve it without the crème fraîche."

"No," I say. "Really, I just couldn't."

We ask for the check, explaining that we have a movie to catch. It's only a ten-minute walk to the theater, but I'm antsy because I'd like to get something to eat before the show. They'll have loads of food at the concession stand, but I don't believe in mixing meat with my movies. Luckily there's a hot dog cart not too far out of our way.

Friends always say, "How can you eat those? I read in the paper that they're made from hog's lips."

"And . . . ?"

"And hearts and eyelids."

That, to my mind, is only three ingredients and constitutes a refreshing change of pace. I order mine with nothing but mustard, and am thrilled to watch the vendor present my hot dog in a horizontal position. So simple and timeless that I can recognize it, immediately, as food.

City of Angels

My CHILDHOOD FRIEND ALISHA LIVES in North Carolina but used to visit me in New York at least twice a year. She was always an easy, undemanding houseguest, and it was a pleasure having her as she was happy following me around on errands or just lying on my sofa reading a magazine. "Just pretend I'm not here," she'd say — and I sometimes did. Quiet and willing to do whatever anyone else wanted, she was often favorably compared to a shadow.

A week before one of her regular December visits, Alisha called to say that she'd be bringing along a guest, someone named Bonnie. The woman worked at a sandwich shop and had never traveled more than fifty miles from her home in Greensboro. Alisha hadn't known her long but said that she seemed like a very sweet person. That's one of Alisha's most well-worn adjectives, *sweet,* and she uses it to describe just about everyone. Were you to kick her in the stomach, the most you could expect would be a demotion to "semi sweet." I've never known anyone so willing to withhold judgment and overlook what often strike me as major personality defects. Like all of my friends, she's a lousy judge of character.

The two women arrived in New York on a Friday afternoon, and upon greeting them, I noticed an uncommon expression on Alisha's face. It was the look of someone who's discovered too late that she's either set her house on fire or committed herself to traveling with the wrong person. "Run for your life," she whispered.

Bonnie was a dour, spindly woman whose thick girlish braids fell like leashes over the innocent puppies pictured on her sweatshirt. She had a pronounced Greensboro accent and had landed at Kennedy convinced that, given half a chance, the people of New York would steal the fillings right out of her mouth — and she was not about to let that happen.

"The cabdriver said, 'It sounds to me like you two ladies are from out of town,' and I knew right then that he was planning to rip us off."

Alisha placed her head in her hands, massaging what had become a visible headache.

"I knew exactly what he was up to. I know the rules, I'm not stupid, so I wrote down his name and license number and said I'd report him to the police if he tried any funny business. I didn't come all this way to be robbed blind, and I told him that, didn't I, Alisha?"

She showed me the taxi receipt, and I assured her that this was indeed the correct price. It was a standard thirty-dollar fare from Kennedy Airport to any destination in Manhattan.

She stuffed the receipt back into her wallet. "Well, I hope he wasn't expecting a tip, because he didn't get a dime out of me."

"You didn't tip him?"

"Hell no!" Bonnie said. "I don't know about you, but I work hard for my money. It's mine and I'm not tipping anybody unless they give me the kind of service I expect."

"Fine," I said. "But what kind of service did you expect if you've never ridden in a cab before?"

"I expect to be treated like everybody else is what I expect. I expect to be treated like an American."

That was the root of the problem right there. Visiting Americans will find more warmth in Tehran than they will in New York, a city founded on the principle of Us versus Them. I don't speak Latin but have always assumed that the city motto translates to either Go Home or We Don't Like You, Either. Like me, most of the people I knew had moved to New York with the express purpose of escaping Americans such as Bonnie. Fear had worked in our favor until a new mayor began promoting the city as a family theme park. His campaign had worked, and now the Bonnies were arriving in droves, demanding the same hospitality they'd received last month in Orlando.

I've had visitors from all over, but Alisha's friend was the first to arrive with an itinerary, a thick bundle of brochures and schedules she kept in a nylon pouch strapped around her waist. Before leaving North Carolina, she'd spoken to a travel agent who'd provided her with a list of destinations anyone in her right mind would know to avoid, especially around the holidays, when the crowds multiply to Chinese proportions.

"Well," I said, "we'll see what we can do. I'm sure Alisha has places she'd like to go, too, so maybe we can just take turns."

The expression on her face suggested that give-and-take was a new and unpleasant concept to Bonnie of Greensboro. Her jaw tightened, and she turned back to her brochures, muttering, "I came to New York to see New York and isn't nobody going to stop me."

Our troubles began the following morning when I disregarded the itinerary and took the two women to the Chelsea flea market. Alisha wanted to look for records and autographs. Bonnie wasn't much of a shopper, but after a pronounced bout of whining, she decided she wouldn't mind adding to her lifelong angel collection. Angels, she said, were God's way of saying howdy.

The flea market was good for records and autographs, but none of the angels mustered an appropriate howdy. "Not at these prices. I asked some lady how much she wanted for a little glass angel playing a trumpet, and when she said it cost forty-five dollars, I told her to go straight to you know where. I said there's no way I'm paying that much when back home I can get ten angels for half that price. 'And,' I said, 'they'd be a lot more spiritual than the sorry-looking New York angels y'all have here.' That's exactly what I told her."

She pronounced the flea market a complete waste of

time, adding that she was cold and hungry and ready to leave. It was decided that even though $1.50 was a lot to charge for a ten-minute ride, we would take the subway uptown and get something to eat. Things went smoothly until the transit clerk accidentally shorted her a nickle and Bonnie stuck her mouth into the token window, shouting, "Excuse me, but for your information, I do not appreciate being taken for a fool. I may be from Greensboro, North Carolina, but I can count just as well as anyone else. Now, are you going to give me my five cents, or should I talk to your supervisor?"

At the restaurant she insisted that the waitress had over-charged her for her milk shake, even though the price was right there on the menu. When I suggested we leave and maybe see a movie, Bonnie pushed herself back from the table and proceeded to sulk. "I wanted to go to a Broadway show, and here you're talking about a movie I could see back home for three dollars and fifty cents. I flew five hundred miles to see New York, and all I got was a chocolate milk shake and a plate of hash browns. Some damn trip this turned out to be."

We should have beaten her to death. It was clearly the best solution to the problem, but instead we went to the half-price ticket booth. Alisha took her monster to a Broadway show, and I met up with them afterward. We hoped the play might satisfy Bonnie, but once she'd gotten a taste of her itin-erary, there was no stopping her. The following morning she woke Alisha at seven A.M. so they could get a head start on the Statue of Liberty and the Empire State Building. They visited the UN and the South Street Seaport and returned to the apartment at four in the afternoon. Alisha was ready to throw in the towel, but Bonnie wanted to go for high tea at the Plaza Hotel. High tea is fine if you like that sort of thing, but she became angry when I suggested that she might first want to change into something more appropriate. The woman was wearing what people in the South refer to as "hog washers," the sort of denim overalls favored by farmers. The crowd at the Plaza would most likely be dressed up, and I worried that she might feel out of place in an outfit most people associate with hard manual labor. I was only trying to help, but Bonnie didn't see it that way.

"Let me tell you something, Mr. New York City. I am very comfortable with the way I look, and if the Plaza Hotel doesn't like what I'm wearing, then that's *their* problem, not mine."

I'd done my best to warn her but was actually thrilled when she rejected my advice. The scarecrow look was fine by me. I'd never been to the Plaza but felt certain she'd be eaten alive by troops of wealthy, overcaffeinated society women with high standards and excellent aim. Service would be denied, voices would be raised, and she'd wind up drinking her tea at some pancake restaurant in midtown. Alisha changed into a dress, and I dropped them off at the hotel, returning an hour later to find Bonnie wandering the tearoom with her disposable camera. "Would y'all mind taking a picture of me standing next to the waiter? I'd have my friend do it, but she's got a bug up her butt."

I expected her to be physically removed from the building and was horrified to realize that the Plaza Hotel was essentially Bonnie Central. Dressed for comfort in sweatshirts and tracksuits, her fellow scarecrows were more than happy to accommodate her. The flashbulbs were blinding.

"Now those were some nice New Yorkers," she said, waving good-bye to the crowd in the tearoom. I tried to explain that they weren't real New Yorkers, but at that point she'd stopped listening to anything I had to say. She dragged Alisha off for a carriage ride through Central Park, and then it was time for a visit to what she called "Fay-o Schwartz." The toy store was followed by brutal pilgrimages to Radio City Music Hall, St. Patrick's Cathedral, and the Christmas tree at Rockefeller Plaza. The crowds were such that you could pick your feet off the ground and be carried for blocks in either direction. I was mortified, but Bonnie was in a state of almost narcotic bliss, overjoyed to have discovered a New York without the New Yorkers. Here were out-of-town visitors from Omaha and Chattanooga, outraged over the price of their hot roasted chestnuts. They apologized when stepping on someone's foot and never thought to complain when some nitwit with a video camera stupidly blocked their path. The crowd was relentlessly, pathologically friendly, and their enthusiasm was deafening. Looking around her, Bonnie saw a glittering paradise filled with decent, like-minded people, sent by God to give the world a howdy. Encircled by her army of angels, she drifted across the avenue to photograph a juggler, while I hobbled off toward home, a clear outsider in a city I'd foolishly thought to call my own.

A Shiner

Like a Diamond

I'D BEEN LIVING IN MANHATTAN for eight years when my father called, excited by the news that my sister Amy was scheduled to appear in a magazine article devoted to the subject of interesting New York women.

"Can you imagine?" he asked. "My God, put a camera in front of that girl, and she'll shine like a diamond! Between the single men and the job opportunities, her phone is going to be ringing right off the hook!" He paused for a moment, perhaps imagining the life of a young New York woman whose phone rings off the hook. "We just have to make sure that none of the wrong people call her. You'll take care of that, right?"

"I'm putting it on my to-do list as we speak."

"Good boy," he said. "The trouble is that she's just so

darn pretty. That's the danger right there. Plus, you know, she's a girl."

My father has always placed a great deal of importance on his daughters' physical beauty. It is, to him, their greatest asset, and he monitors their appearance with the intensity of a pimp. What can I say? He was born a long time ago and is convinced that marriage is a woman's only real shot at happiness. Because it was always assumed that we would lead professional lives, my brother and I were free to grow as plump and ugly as we liked. Our bodies were viewed as mere vehicles, pasty, potbellied machines designed to transport our thoughts from one place to another. I might wander freely through the house drinking pancake batter from a plastic bucket, but the moment one of my sisters overspilled her bikini, my father was right there to mix his metaphors. "Jesus, Flossie, what are we running here, a dairy farm? Look at you, you're the size of a house. Two more pounds, and you won't be able to cross state lines without a trucking license."

"Oh, Lou," my mother would moan, "for Christ's sake, give it a rest."

"Aw, baloney. They'll thank me for this later." He honestly thought he was doing his girls a favor, and it confused him when the thanks never came.

In response to his vigilance and pressure, my sisters grew increasingly defensive and self-conscious. The sole exception turned out to be Amy, who is capable of getting even without first getting mad. Nothing seems to stick to her, partly because she's so rarely herself. Her fondness for transformation began at an early age and has developed into something closely resembling a multiple personality disorder. She's Sybil with a better sense of humor, Eve without the crying jags. "And who are we today?" my mother used to ask, leading to Amy's "Who don't you want me to be?"

At the age of ten Amy was caught taking a fistful of twenties from an unguarded till at the grocery store. I was with her and marveled at my sister's deftness and complete lack of fear. When the manager was called, she calmly explained that she wasn't stealing, she was simply pretending to be a thief. "And thieves steal," she said. "So that's what I was doing." It all made perfect sense to her.

She failed first grade by pretending to be stupid, but the setback didn't seem to bother her. For Amy school was devoted solely to the study of her teachers. She meticulously charted the repetition of their shoes and earrings and was quick to pinpoint their mannerisms. After school, alone in her simulated classroom, she would talk like them, dress like them, and assign herself homework she would never complete.

She became a Girl Scout only to become her Girl Scout leader. For Christmases and birthdays she requested wigs and makeup, hospital gowns and uniforms. Amy became my mother, and then my mother's friends. She was great as Sooze Grossman and Eleanor Kelliher, but her best impersonation was of Penny Midland, a stylish fifty-year-old woman who worked part-time at an art gallery my parents visited on a regular basis. Penny's voice was deep and roughly textured. She wasn't shy, but when she spoke, certain words tended to leave her mouth reluctantly, as if they'd been forced out against their will.

Dressed in a caftan and an appropriate white pageboy wig, Amy began phoning my father at the office. "Lou Sedaris! Penny Midland here. How the . . . hell are you?"

Surprised that this woman would be calling him at work, our father feigned enthusiasm as best he could. "Penny! Well, what do you know. Gosh, it's good to hear your voice."

The first few times she called, Amy discussed gallery business but, little by little, began complaining about her husband, a Westinghouse executive named Van. There were problems at home. Her marriage, it seemed, was on the rocks.

Our father offered comfort with his standard noncommittal phrases, reminding Penny that there were two sides to every coin and that it's always darkest before the dawn.

"Oh, Lou. It just feels so good to . . . talk to someone who really . . . understands."

I walked into the kitchen late one afternoon and came upon my twelve-year-old sister propositioning our father with lines she'd collected from *Guiding Light*. "I think we've both seen this coming for a long . . . time. The only question left is . . . what are we going to do about it? Oh, baby, let's run wild."

This is what my mother meant when she accused people of playing a dangerous game. Were our father to accept Penny's offer, Amy would have known him as a philanderer and wondered who else he might have slept with. Everything he'd ever said would be shaded by doubt and called into question. Was that *really* a business trip, or had he snuck off to Myrtle Beach with one of the Strivides twins? Who *was* this man?

Amy studied her reflection in the oven door, arranging her white bangs and liking what she saw. "All I'm saying is that I find you to be a very attractive . . . man. Is that such . . . a crime?"

It is to his credit that our father was such a gentleman. Stammering that he was very flattered to be asked, he let Penny down as gently as possible. After offering to set her up with some available bachelors from his office and country club, he told my sister to take care of herself, adding that she was a very special woman who deserved to be happy.

It was years before Amy finally admitted what she had done. They were relatively uneventful years for our family but, I imagine, a very confusing period of time for poor Penny Midland, who was frequently visited at the art gallery by my father and any number of his divorced associates. "Here's the gal I was telling you about," he'd say. "Why don't I just take a look around and give you two a chance to talk."

The passage of time has not altered my father's obsessive attention to my sisters' weight and appearance. He wonders why the girls don't drop by more often, and then when they do, he opens the door asking, "Is it just my imagination, or have you put on a few pounds?"

Because she has maintained her beautiful skin and enviable figure, Amy remains my father's greatest treasure. She is by far the most attractive member of the family, yet she spends most of her time and money disguising herself beneath prosthetic humps and appliquéd skin diseases. She's got more neck braces and false teeth than she knows what to do with, and her drawers and closets overflow with human hair. Having dreamt of one for years, she finally broke down and bought half of a padded, custom-made "fatty suit," which she enjoys wearing beneath dirty sweatpants as tight and uninviting as sausage casings. Unable to afford the suit's matching top, she's been reduced to waddling the streets much like two women fused together in some sort of cruel experiment. From the waist up she's slim and fit, chugging forward on legs the size of tree trunks and followed by a wide, dimpled bottom so thick that she could sit on a knitting needle and never feel a thing.

She wore the fatty suit home one Christmas, and our father met us at the Raleigh airport. Visibly shaken, he managed to say nothing on the short ride to the house, but the moment Amy stepped into the bathroom he turned to me, shouting, "What the hell happened to her? Christ almighty, this is killing me! I'm in real pain here."

"What?"

"Your sister, that's what. I just saw her six months ago,

and now the girl's the size of a tank! I thought you were supposed to be keeping an eye on her."

I begged him to lower his voice. "Please, Dad, don't mention it in front of her. Amy's very sensitive about her . . . you know."

"Her what? Go ahead and say it: *her big, fat ass*. That's what she's ashamed of, and she should be! You could land a chopper on an ass like that."

"Oh, Dad."

"Don't try to defend her, wiseguy. She's a single woman, and the clock is ticking away. Who's going to love her, who's going to marry her with an ass like that?"

"Well," I said, "from what I've been told, a lot of men *prefer* rear ends like that."

He looked at me with great pity, his heart breaking for the second time that day. "Man, what you don't know could fill a book."

My father composed himself when Amy re-entered the room, but when she turned to open the refrigerator door, he acted as though she were tossing a lit match into the gas tank of his Porsche. "What in God's name are you doing? Look at you — you're killing yourself."

Amy stuck a tablespoon into an economy-size vat of mayonnaise.

"Your problem is that you're bored," my father said. "You're bored and lonely and you're eating garbage to fill the void. I know what you're going through, but believe me, you can beat this."

Amy denied that she was bored and lonely. The problem, she said, was that she was hungry. "All I had on the plane were a couple of Danish. Can we go out for pancakes?"

She kept it up until our father, his voice cracking with pain, offered to find her some professional help. He mentioned camps and personal trainers, offering to loan — no, *give* — her the money, "And on top of that, I'll pay you for every pound you take off."

When Amy rejected his offer, he attempted to set an example. His Christmas dinner was gone in three bites, and dessert was skipped in favor of a brisk two-mile run. "Anyone want to join me? Amy?" He extended his age-old exercise regimen from ten minutes to an hour and trotted in place while speaking on the telephone.

Amy kept to her fatty suit until her legs were chafed and pimpled. It was on the morning of our return flight that she finally revealed her joke, and our father wept with relief. "Ha-ha, you really had me going. I should have known you'd never do that to yourself. And it's really fake? Ha-ha."

He reflected upon the fatty suit for the next several months. "She had me fooled for a minute there, but even with a big, fat ass she can't disguise the fact that she's a beautiful person, both inside and out, and that's what really matters." His epiphany was short-lived, and as the photo shoot approached, he began calling me with technical questions. "Do you happen to know if this magazine will be hiring a professional beautician? I sure as hell hope so, because her hair is getting awfully thin. And what are they going to do about lighting? Can we trust the photographer to do a first-class job, or should we call and see if they can't come up with someone better?

There's a lot I don't tell my father when he calls asking after Amy. He wouldn't understand that she has no interest in getting married and was, in fact, quite happy to break up with her live-in boyfriend, whom she replaced with an imaginary boyfriend named Ricky.

The last time she was asked out by a successful bachelor, Amy hesitated before saying, "Thanks for asking, but I'm really not into white guys right now."

That alone would have stopped my father's heartbeat. "The clock is ticking," he says. "If she waits much longer, she'll be alone for the rest of her life."

This appears to suit Amy just fine.

When my father phoned asking about the photo shoot, I pretended to know nothing. I didn't tell him that, at the scheduled time, my sister arrived at the studio with unwashed hair and took a seat beside the dozen other New York women selected by the magazine. She complimented them on their flattering, carefully chosen outfits and waited as they had their hair fashioned, their eyebrows trained, and their slight imperfections masked by powder.

When it was her turn at the styling table, Amy said, "I want to look like someone has beaten the shit out of me."

The makeup artist did a fine job. The black eyes and purple jaw were accentuated by an arrangement of scratch marks on her forehead. Pus-yellow pools girdled her scabbed nose, and her swollen lips were fenced with mean rows of brackish stitches.

Amy adored both the new look and the new person it allowed her to be. Following the photo shoot, she wore her bruises to the dry cleaner and the grocery store. Most people nervously looked away, but on the rare occasions someone would ask what happened, my sister would smile as brightly as possible, saying, "I'm in love. Can you believe it? I'm finally, totally in love, and I feel great."

Nutcracker.com

It was my father's dream that one day the people of the world would be connected to one another through a network of blocky, refrigerator-size computers, much like those he was helping develop at IBM. He envisioned families of the future gathered around their mammoth terminals, ordering groceries and paying their taxes from the comfort of their own homes. A person could compose music, design a doghouse, and . . . something more, something even better. "A person could . . . he could . . ."

When predicting this utopia, he would eventually reach a point where words failed him. His eyes would widen and sparkle at the thought of this indescribable something more. "I mean, my God," he'd say, "just think about it."

My sisters and I preferred not to. I didn't know about

them, but I was hoping the people of the world might be united by something more interesting, like drugs or an armed struggle against the undead. Unfortunately, my father's team won, so computers it is. My only regret is that this had to happen during my lifetime.

Somewhere in the back of my mind is a dim memory of standing in some line holding a perforated card. I remember the cheap, slightly clinical feeling it gave me, and recall thinking that the computer would never advance much further than this. Call me naive, but I seem to have underestimated the universal desire to sit in a hard plastic chair and stare at a screen until your eyes cross. My father saw it coming, but this was a future that took me completely by surprise. There were no computers in my high school, and the first two times I attempted college, people were still counting on their fingers and removing their shoes when the numbers got above ten. I wasn't really aware of computers until the mid-1980s. For some reason, I seemed to know quite a few graphic designers whose homes and offices pleasantly stank of Spray Mount. Their floors were always collaged with stray bits of paper, and trapped flies waved for help from the gummy killing fields of their tabletops. I had always counted on these friends to loan me the adhesive of my choice, but then, seemingly overnight, their Scotch tape and rubber cement were gone, replaced with odorless computers and spongy mouse pads. They had nothing left that I wanted to borrow, and so I dropped them and fell in with a group of typesetters who ultimately betrayed me as well.

Thanks to my complete lack of office skills, I found it fairly easy to avoid direct contact with the new technology. The indirect contact was disturbing enough. I was still living in Chicago when I began to receive creepy Christmas newsletters designed to look like tabloids and annual reports. Word processors made writing fun. They did not, however, make reading fun, a point made painfully evident by such publications as *The Herald Family Tribune* and *Wassup with the Wexlers!*

Friends who had previously expressed no interest in torture began sending letters composed to resemble Chinese take-out menus and the Dead Sea Scrolls. Everybody had a font, and I was told that I should get one, too. The authors of these letters shared an enthusiasm with the sort of people who now arrived at dinner parties hoisting expensive new video cameras and suggesting that, after dessert, we all sit down and replay the evening on TV. We, the regular people of the world, now had access to the means of production, but still I failed to see what all the fuss was about. A dopey letter is still a dopey letter, no matter how you dress it up; and there's a reason regular people don't appear on TV: we're boring.

By the early 1990s I was living in New York and working for a housecleaning company. My job taught me that regardless of their purported virtues, computers are a pain in the ass to keep clean. The pebbled surface is a magnet for grease and dirt, and you can pretty much forget about reaming out the gaps in the keyboard. More than once I accidentally pushed a button and recoiled in terror as the blank screen came to life with exotic tropical fish or swarms of flying toasters. Equally distressing was the way people used the slanted roofs of their terminals to display framed photographs and great populations of plush and plastic creatures, which would fall behind the desk the moment I began cleaning the screen. There was never any place to plug in the vacuum, as every outlet was occupied by some member of the computer family. Cords ran wild, and everyone seemed to own one of those ominous foot-long power strips with the blinking red light that sends the message YOU MUST LEAVE US ALONE. I was more than happy to comply, and the complaints came rolling in.

Due to my general aversion to machines and a few pronounced episodes of screaming, I was labeled a technophobe, a term that ranks fairly low on my scale of fightin' words. The word *phobic* has its place when properly used, but lately it's been declawed by the pompous insistence that most animosity is based upon fear rather than loathing. No credit is given for distinguishing between these two very different emotions. I fear snakes. I hate computers. My hatred is entrenched, and I nourish it daily. I'm comfortable with it, and no community outreach program will change my mind.

I hate computers for getting their own section in the *New York Times* and for lengthening commercials with the mention of a web site address. Who really wants to find out more about Procter & Gamble? Just buy the toothpaste or laundry detergent, and get on with it. I hate them for creating the word *org* and I hate them for e-mail, which isn't real mail but a variation of the pointless notes people used to pass in class.

I hate computers for replacing the card catalog in the New York Public Library and I hate the way they've invaded the movies. I'm not talking about their contribution to the world of special effects. I have nothing against a well-defined mutant or full-scale alien invasion — that's *good* technology. I'm talking about their actual presence *in* any given movie. They've become like horses in a western — they may not be the main focus, but everybody seems to have one. Each tiresome new thriller includes a scene in which the hero, trapped by some version of the enemy, runs for his desk in a desperate race against time. Music swells and droplets of sweat rain down on to the keyboard as he sits at his laptop, frantically pawing for answers. It might be different if he were flagging down a passing car or trying to phone for help, but typing, in and of itself, is not an inherently dramatic activity.

I hate computers for any number of reasons, but I despise them most for what they've done to my friend the typewriter. In a democratic country you'd think there would be room for both of them, but computers won't rest until I'm making my ribbons from torn shirts and brewing Wite-Out in my bathtub. Their goal is to place the IBM Selectric II beside the feather quill and chisel in the museum of antiquated writing implements. They're power hungry, and someone needs to stop them.

When told I'm like the guy still pining for his eight-track tapes, I say, "You have eight-tracks? Where?" In reality I know nothing about them, yet I feel it's important to express some solidarity with others who have had the rug pulled out from beneath them. I don't care if it can count words or rearrange paragraphs at the push of a button, I don't want a computer. Unlike the faint scurry raised by fingers against a plastic computer keyboard, the smack and clatter of a typewriter suggests that you're actually building something. At the end of a miserable day, instead of grieving my virtual nothing, I can always look at my loaded wastepaper basket and tell myself that if I failed, at least I took a few trees down with me.

When forced to leave my house for an extended period of time, I take my typewriter with me, and together we endure the wretchedness of passing through the X-ray scanner. The laptops roll merrily down the belt, while I'm instructed to stand aside and open my bag. To me it seems like a normal enough thing to be carrying, but the typewriter's declining popularity arouses suspicion and I wind up eliciting the sort of reaction one might expect when traveling with a cannon.

"It's a typewriter," I say. "You use it to write angry letters to airport authorities."

The keys are then slapped and pounded, and I'm forced to explain that if you want the words to appear, you first have to plug it in and insert a sheet of paper.

The goons shake their heads and tell me I really should be using a computer. That's their job, to stand around in an ill-fitting uniform and tell you how you should lead your life. I'm told the exact same thing later in the evening when the bellhop knocks on my hotel door. The people whose televisions I can hear have complained about my typing, and he has come to make me stop. To hear him talk, you'd think I'd been playing the kettledrum. In the great scheme of things, the typewriter is not nearly as loud as he makes it out to be, but there's no use arguing with him. "You know," he says, "you really should be using a computer."

You have to wonder where you've gone wrong when twice a day you're offered writing advice from men in funny hats. The harder I'm pressured to use a computer, the harder I resist. One by one, all of my friends have deserted me and fled to the dark side. "How can I write to you if you don't have an e-mail address?" they ask. They talk of their B-trees and Disk Doctors and then have the nerve to complain when I discuss bowel obstructions at the dinner table.

Who needs them? I think. I figured I'd always have my family and was devastated when my sister Amy brought home a candy-colored laptop. "I only use it for e-mail," she said. Coming from her, these words made me physically ill. "It's fun," she said. "People send you things. Look at this." She pushed a button, and there, on the screen, was a naked man lying facedown on a carpet. His hair was graying and his hands were cuffed behind his doughy back. A woman entered the room. You couldn't see her face, just her legs and feet, which were big and mean-looking, forced into sharp-toed shoes with high, pencil-thin heels. The man on the carpet shifted position, and when his testicles came into view, the woman reacted as if she had seen an old balding mouse, one that she had been trying to kill for a long time. She stomped on the man's testicles with the toes of her shoes and then she turned around and stomped on them with the heels. She kicked them mercilessly and, just when I thought she'd finished, she got her second wind and started all over again.

I'd never realized that a computer could act so much like a TV set. No one had ever told me that the picture could be so clear, that the cries of pain could be heard so distinctly. This, I thought, was what my father had been envisioning all those years ago when words had failed him, not necessarily this scene, but something equally capable of provoking such wonder.

"Again?" Amy pushed a button and, our faces bathed in the glow of the screen, we watched the future a second time.

*Deux**

See You Again
Yesterday

I HAVE NEVER BEEN ONE of those Americans who pepper their conversation with French phrases and entertain guests with wheels of brie. For me, France was never a specific, premeditated destination. I wound up in Normandy the same way my mother wound up in North Carolina: you meet a guy, relinquish a tiny bit of control, and the next thing you know, you're eating a different part of the pig.

I met Hugh through a mutual friend. She and I were painting an apartment, and he had offered the use of his twelve-foot ladder. Owning a twelve-foot ladder in New York is a probable sign of success, as it means you most likely have enough room to store one. At the time, Hugh was living in a loft on Canal Street, a former chocolate factory where the walk-in coolers had been turned into bedrooms. I arrived at his place on a Friday night and noticed the pie baking in the oven. While the rest of Manhattan was out on the town, he'd stayed home to peel apples and listen to country music.

Like me, Hugh was single, which came as no great surprise, considering that he spent his leisure time rolling out dough and crying to George Jones albums. I had just moved to New York and was wondering if I was going to be alone for the rest of my life. Part of the problem was that, according to several reliable sources, I tended to exhaust people. Another part of the problem had to do with my long list of standards. Potential boyfriends could not smoke Merit cigarettes, own or wear a pair of cowboy boots, or eat anything labeled either *lite* or *heart smart*. Speech was important, and disqualifying phrases included "I can't find my nipple ring" and "This one here was my *first* tattoo." All street names had to be said in full, meaning no "Fifty-ninth and Lex," and definitely no "Mad Ave." They couldn't drink more than I did, couldn't write poetry in notebooks and read it out loud to an audience of strangers, and couldn't use the words *flick, freebie, cyberspace, progressive,* or *zeitgeist.* They could not consider the human scalp an appropriate palette for self-expression, could not own a rainbow-striped flag, and could not say they had "discovered" any shop or restaurant currently listed in the phone book. Age, race, and weight were unimportant. In terms of mutual interests, I figured we could spend the rest of our lives discussing how much we hated the aforementioned characteristics.

Hugh had moved to New York after spending six years in

France. I asked a few questions, rightly sensing that he probably wouldn't offer anything unless provoked. There was, he said, a house in Normandy. This was most likely followed by a qualifier, something pivotal like "but it's a dump." He probably described it in detail, but by that point I was only half listening. Instead, I'd begun to imagine my life in a foreign country, some faraway land where, if things went wrong, I could always blame somebody else, saying I'd never wanted to live there in the first place. Life might be difficult for a year or two, but I would tough it out because living in a foreign country is one of those things that everyone should try at least once. My understanding was that it completed a person, sanding down the rough provincial edges and transforming you into a citizen of the world.

I didn't see this as a romantic idea. It had nothing to do with France itself, with wearing hats or writing tortured letters from a sidewalk café. I didn't care where Hemingway drank or Alice B. Toklas had her mustache trimmed. What I found appealing in life abroad was the inevitable sense of helplessness it would inspire. Equally exciting would be the work involved in overcoming that helplessness. There would be a goal involved, and I like having goals.

"Built around 1780 . . . a two-hour train ride from Paris . . . the neighbor keeps his horses in my backyard . . . pies made with apples from my own trees . . ."

I caught the highlights of Hugh's broadcast and understood that my first goal was to make him my boyfriend, to trick or blackmail him into making some sort of commitment.

I know it sounds calculating, but if you're not cute, you might as well be clever.

In order to get the things I want, it helps me to pretend I'm a figure in a daytime drama, a schemer. Soap opera characters make emphatic pronouncements. They ball up their fists and state their goals out loud. "I *will* destroy Buchanan Enterprises," they say. "Phoebe Wallingford *will* pay for what she's done to our family." Walking home with the back half of the twelve-foot ladder, I turned to look in the direction of Hugh's loft. "You *will* be mine," I commanded.

Nine months after I'd borrowed the ladder, Hugh left the chocolate factory and we moved in together. As was his habit, he planned to spend the month of August in Normandy, visiting friends and working on his house. I'd planned to join him, but that first year, when the time came to buy my ticket, I chickened out, realizing that I was afraid of France. My fear had nothing to do with the actual French people. I didn't know any actual French people. What scared me was the idea of French people I'd gotten from movies and situation comedies. When someone makes a spectacular ass of himself, it's always in a French restaurant, never a Japanese or Italian one. The French are the people who slap one another with gloves and wear scarves to cover their engorged hickies. My understanding was that, no matter how hard we tried, the French would never like us, and that's confusing to an American raised to believe that the citizens of Europe should be grateful for all the wonderful things we've done. Things like movies that stereotype the people of France as boors and petty snobs, and little remarks such as "We saved your ass in World War II." Every day we're told that we live in the greatest country on earth. And it's always stated as an undeniable fact: Leos are born between July 23 and August 22, fitted queen-size sheets measure sixty by eighty inches, and America is the greatest country on earth. Having grown up with this in our ears, it's startling to realize that other countries have nationalistic slogans of their own, none of which are "We're number two!"

The French have decided to ignore our self-proclaimed superiority, and this is translated as arrogance. To my knowledge, they've never said that they're better than us; they've just never said that we're the best. Big deal. There are plenty of places on earth where visiting Americans are greeted with great enthusiasm. Unfortunately, these places tend to lack anything you'd really want to buy. And that, to me, is the only reason to leave home in the first place — to buy things. Hugh bought me great gifts the summer I stayed home and he went off to France. He's not really that much of a shopper, so I figured that if he had managed to find these things, they must have been right out in the open where anyone could have spotted them. As far as I was concerned, the French could be cold or even openly hostile. They could burn my flag or pelt me with stones, but if there were taxidermied kittens to be had, then I would go and bring them back to this, the greatest country on earth.

There was the shopping, and then there was the smoking. Hugh returned from his trip, and days later I still sounded like a Red Chinese asking questions about the democratic hinterlands. "And you actually saw people smoking in restaurants? Really! And offices, too? Oh, tell me again about the ashtrays in the hospital waiting room, and don't leave anything out."

I went to France the following summer knowing only the word for *bottleneck*. I said "bottleneck" at the airport, "bottleneck" on the train to Normandy, and "bottleneck" when presented with the pile of stones that was Hugh's house in the country. There was no running water, no electricity, and nothing to buy but the pipes and wires needed if you wanted to live with plumbing and electricity. Because there was nothing decent to buy, the people greeted me with great enthusiasm. It would be the same if a French person were to visit, say, Knightdale, North Carolina. "My goodness," everyone said, "you came all this way to see us?"

Had my vocabulary been larger, I might have said, "Well, no, not exactly." Times being what they were, I offered my only possible response. "Bottleneck."

"Oh, bottleneck," everyone said. "You speak very well."

They were nothing like the French people I had imagined. If anything, they were too kind, too generous, and too knowledgeable in the fields of plumbing and electricity. The house is located in a tiny hamlet, a Hooterville of eight stone houses huddled in a knot and surrounded by rolling hills decorated with cows and sheep. There are no cash registers, but a mile away, in the neighboring village, there's a butcher, a baker, a post office, a hardware store, and a small grocery.

There's a church and a pay phone, an elementary school, and a place to buy cigarettes. "New York City!" the shopkeepers said. "Well, you're far from home, aren't you?" They said this as if I'd left Manhattan for a short walk and lost track of the time.

It seemed that if you had to be from America, New York was as good a place as any. People had heard of it, especially the three village teenagers who studied English in school and often dropped by to discuss life in what they called, "Ny." I tried to explain that the N and the Y were initials that stood for *New* and *York*, but still they insisted on joining the letters into a single word. Ny, they said, was what the insiders called it. Didn't everyone in Usa use that word?

The teenagers were under the impression that New York was a glamorous wonderland, a celebrity playground where one couldn't leave the house without running into Madonna and Michael Jackson sitting in the park and breastfeeding their babies. I thoughtlessly named a few of the stars I had seen in my neighborhood, and for the rest of the summer, when describing our house, you'd say, "It's the place with all the teenagers lying around out front." They stretched out in the middle of the road, flat on their backs, not wanting to miss anything should one of my celebrity friends decide to drop by and help me dig the septic tank. I was afraid that one of them might get hit by a car and that I would be blamed for the death. "Oh, don't worry," the neighbors said. "They'll grow out of it in a few years."

That is what I'm assuming they said. Without Hugh by

my side to translate, every interaction was based upon a series of assumptions. The kind butcher may not have been kind at all, and the grocer might have been saying, "To hell with you and your bottleneck. Go away now and leave me alone." Their personalities were entirely my own invention. On the downside, my personality was entirely their invention. I seemed to have reached my mid-thirties only to be known as "the guy who says 'bottleneck,'" the pied piper who convinces young people to lie in the road, the grown man who ignores the electric-fence warnings and frightens the horses with his screaming. Were such a person described to me, I'd say, "Oh, you mean the village idiot."

In this situation, pretending to be a soap opera character failed to help. When told, "You *will* understand me," the citizens of France responded with blank stares. I picked up a few new words, but the overall situation seemed hopeless. Neighbors would drop by while Hugh was off at the hardware store, and I'd struggle to entertain them with a pathetic series of simple nouns. "Ashtray!"

"Yes," they'd agree. "That's an ashtray all right."

"Hammer? Screwdriver?"

"No, that's okay, we've got our own at home."

I'd hoped the language might come on its own, the way it comes to babies, but people don't talk to foreigners the way they talk to babies. They don't hypnotize you with bright objects and repeat the same words over and over, handing out little treats when you finally say "potty" or "wawa." It got to the point where I'd see a baby in the bakery or grocery store and instinctively ball up my fists, jealous over how easy he had it. I wanted to lie in a French crib and start from scratch, learning the language from the ground floor up. I wanted to be a baby, but instead, I was an adult who talked like one, a spooky man-child demanding more than his fair share of attention.

Rather than admit defeat, I decided to change goals. I told myself that I'd never really cared about learning the language. My main priority was to get the house in shape. The verbs would come in due time, but until then I needed a comfortable place to hide. When eventually developed, our vacation pictures looked as though they had been taken at a forced-labor camp. I knocked down walls and lugged heavy beams, ran pipes and wires, and became a familiar dust-masked face at both the dump and the pharmacy. My month of hard work was rewarded with four days in Paris, a city where, without even trying, one can find a two-hundred-year-old wax model of a vagina, complete with human pubic hair. On the plane going home, I was given a Customs form and asked to list all my purchases:

Two-headed-calf skull

Ashtray in the shape of a protracted molar

Somebody's gallstone, labeled and displayed on an elegant stand

A set of eight Limoges dessert plates custom made for a pharmacy and hand-painted with the names of various lethal drugs

Suede fetus complete with umbilical cord

French eye chart that unintentionally includes the word
FAT

Illustrated guides to skin rashes and war wounds

I ran out of room long before I could mention my outdated
surgical instruments. Hugh told me that I was wasting my
time, that they were looking for people who'd bought plati-
num watches, not rusted cranial saws. My customs form was,
for me, a list of reasons to return to France and master the
language. Conversation would be nice, but the true reward
would be the ability to haggle fluently and get my next two-
headed skull for the same price as a normal one.

Back in New York I took full advantage of my status as a
native speaker. I ran my mouth to shop clerks and listened in
on private conversations, realizing I'd gone an entire month
without hearing anyone complain that they were "stressed-
out," a phrase that's always gotten on my nerves. People in
New York love to tell you how exhausted they are. Then they
fall apart when someone says, "Yeah, you look pretty tired." I
kept an eye out for foreigners, the Europeans shopping on my
SoHo street and the cleaning women who'd answer "Poland"
or "El Salvador" when asked a yes-or-no question. I felt that it
was my responsibility to protect these people, to give them directions they didn't want and generally scare them with my
kindness. As an American abroad, you're bolstered by an
innate sense of security. Something goes wrong, and you instinctively think, "We'll just call the embassy and see what

they have to say." People know where America is on the map. They know that it's loud and powerful. With certain other countries there's no such guarantee. "Oh, right, Laos," I once heard someone say to a dinner guest. "Didn't we bomb you a couple of times?"

Hugh and I returned to Normandy the following summer, and I resumed my identity as the village idiot. "See you again yesterday!" I said to the butcher. "Ashtray! Bottleneck!" Again I hid indoors, painting and scraping until my knuckles bled. I left promising to enroll in a French class and then forgot that promise as soon my plane landed back in New York.

On the following trip I sanded the floors and began the practice of learning ten new words a day.

exorcism
facial swelling
death penalty

I found my words in the dictionary, typed them on to index cards, and committed them to memory while on my daily walks to the neighboring village.

slaughterhouse
sea monster
witch doctor

By the end of the month, I'd managed to retain three hundred nouns, none of which proved to be the least bit useful.

The next summer we went to France for six weeks, and I added another 420 words, most of them found in the popular gossip magazine *Voici*. "Man-eater," I'd say. "Gold digger, roustabout, louse."

"Who are you talking about?" my neighbors would ask. "What social climber? Where?"

On my fifth trip to France I limited myself to the words and phrases that people actually use. From the dog owners I learned "Lie down," "Shut up," and "Who shit on this carpet?" The couple across the road taught me to ask questions correctly, and the grocer taught me to count. Things began to come together, and I went from speaking like an evil baby to speaking like a hillbilly. "Is thems the thoughts of cows?" I'd ask the butcher, pointing to the calves' brains displayed in the front window. "I want me some lamb chop with handles on 'em."

By the end of our sixth trip to France, the house was finished and I'd learned a total of 1,564 words. It was an odd sensation to hold my entire vocabulary in my hands, to look back through the stack and recall the afternoon I learned to effectively describe my hangovers. I kept my vocabulary in a wooden box built to house a Napoleonic hat, and worried that if the house caught fire, I'd be back to square one with *bottleneck* and *ashtray* and would lose the intense pleasure I felt whenever I heard somebody use a word I'd come to think of as my own.

When the cranes arrived to build a twelve-story hotel right outside our bedroom window, Hugh and I decided to leave New York for a year or two, just until our resentment died down a little. I'm determined to learn as much French as possible, so we'll take an apartment in Paris, where there are posters and headlines and any number of words waiting to be captured and transcribed on to index cards, where a person can comfortably smoke while making a spectacular ass of himself, and where, when frustrated, I can lie, saying I never wanted to come here in the first place.

Me Talk Pretty
One Day

AT THE AGE OF FORTY-ONE, I am returning to school and have to think of myself as what my French textbook calls "a true debutant." After paying my tuition, I was issued a student ID, which allows me a discounted entry fee at movie theaters, puppet shows, and Festyland, a far-flung amusement park that advertises with billboards picturing a cartoon stegosaurus sitting in a canoe and eating what appears to be a ham sandwich.

I've moved to Paris with hopes of learning the language. My school is an easy ten-minute walk from my apartment, and on the first day of class I arrived early, watching as the returning students greeted one another in the school lobby. Vacations were recounted, and questions were raised concerning mutual friends with names like Kang and Vlatnya. Regardless of their nationalities, everyone spoke in what sounded to me like excellent French. Some accents were better than others, but the students exhibited an ease and confidence I found intimidating.

The first day of class was nerve-racking because I knew I'd be expected to perform. That's the way they do it here — it's everybody into the language pool, sink or swim. The teacher marched in, deeply tanned from a recent vacation, and proceeded to rattle off a series of administrative announcements. I've spent quite a few summers in Normandy, and I took a month-long French class before leaving New York. I'm not completely in the dark, yet I understood only half of what this woman was saying.

"If you have not *meimslsxp* or *lgpdmurct* by this time, then you should not be in this room. Has everyone *apzkiubjxow?* Everyone? Good, we shall begin." She spread out her lesson plan and sighed, saying, "All right, then, who knows the alphabet?"

It was startling because (a) I hadn't been asked that question in a while and (b) I realized, while laughing, that I myself did *not* know the alphabet. They're the same letters, but in France they're pronounced differently. I know the shape of the alphabet but had no idea what it actually sounded like.

"Ahh." The teacher went to the board and sketched the letter *a*. "Do we have anyone in the room whose first name commences with an *ahh?*"

Two Polish Annas raised their hands, and the teacher instructed them to present themselves by stating their names, nationalities, occupations, and a brief list of things they liked and disliked in this world. The first Anna hailed from an industrial town outside of Warsaw and had front teeth the size of tombstones. She worked as a seamstress, enjoyed quiet times with friends, and hated the mosquito.

"Oh, really," the teacher said. "How very interesting. I thought that everyone loved the mosquito, but here, in front of all the world, you claim to detest him. How is it that we've been blessed with someone as unique and original as you? Tell us, please."

The seamstress did not understand what was being said but knew that this was an occasion for shame. Her rabbity mouth huffed for breath, and she stared down at her lap as though the appropriate comeback were stitched somewhere alongside the zipper of her slacks.

The second Anna learned from the first and claimed to love sunshine and detest lies. It sounded like a translation of one of those Playmate of the Month data sheets, the answers always written in the same loopy handwriting: "Turn-ons: Mom's famous five-alarm chili! Turnoffs: insecurity and guys who come on too strong!!!!"

The two Polish Annas surely had clear notions of what they loved and hated, but like the rest of us, they were limited in terms of vocabulary, and this made them appear less than sophisticated. The teacher forged on, and we learned that Carlos, the Argentine bandonion player, loved wine, music, and,

in his words, "making sex with the womens of the world."
Next came a beautiful young Yugoslav who identified herself
as an optimist, saying that she loved everything that life had
to offer.

The teacher licked her lips, revealing a hint of the sadist
we would later come to know. She crouched low for her
attack, placed her hands on the young woman's desk, and
leaned close, saying, "Oh yeah? And do you love your little
war?"

While the optimist struggled to defend herself, I scrambled to think of an answer to what had obviously become a
trick question. How often is one asked what he loves in this
world? More to the point, how often is one asked and then
publicly ridiculed for his answer? I recalled my mother, flushed
with wine, pounding the tabletop late one night, saying,
"Love? I love a good steak cooked rare. I love my cat, and I
love . . ." My sisters and I leaned forward, waiting to hear our
names. "Rennies," our mother said. "I love Rennies."

The teacher killed some time accusing the Yugoslavian
girl of masterminding a program of genocide, and I jotted
frantic notes in the margins of my pad. While I can honestly
say that I love leafing through medical textbooks devoted to
severe dermatological conditions, the hobby is beyond the
reach of my French vocabulary, and acting it out would only
have invited controversy.

When called upon, I delivered an effortless list of things
that I detest: blood sausage, intestinal pâtés, brain pudding.
I'd learned these words the hard way. Having given it some

thought, I then declared my love for IBM typewriters, the French word for *bruise,* and my electric floor waxer. It was a short list, but still I managed to mispronounce *IBM* and assign the wrong gender to both the floor waxer and the typewriter. The teacher's reaction led me to believe that these mistakes were capital crimes in the country of France.

"Were you always this *palicmkrexis?*" she asked. "Even a *fiuscrzsa ticiwelmun* knows that a typewriter is feminine."

I absorbed as much of her abuse as I could understand, thinking — but not saying — that I find it ridiculous to assign a gender to an inanimate object incapable of disrobing and making an occasional fool of itself. Why refer to Lady Crack Pipe or Good Sir Dishrag when these things could never live up to all that their sex implied?

The teacher proceeded to belittle everyone from German Eva, who hated laziness, to Japanese Yukari, who loved paintbrushes and soap. Italian, Thai, Dutch, Korean, and Chinese — we all left class foolishly believing that the worst was over. She'd shaken us up a little, but surely that was just an act designed to weed out the deadweight. We didn't know it then, but the coming months would teach us what it was like to spend time in the presence of a wild animal, something completely unpredictable. Her temperament was not based on a series of good and bad days but, rather, good and bad moments. We soon learned to dodge chalk and protect our heads and stomachs whenever she approached us with a question. She hadn't yet punched anyone, but it seemed wise to protect ourselves against the inevitable.

Though we were forbidden to speak anything but French, the teacher would occasionally use us to practice any of her five fluent languages.

"I hate you," she said to me one afternoon. Her English was flawless. "I really, really hate you." Call me sensitive, but I couldn't help but take it personally.

After being singled out as a lazy *kfɑ̃tinvfm*, I took to spending four hours a night on my homework, putting in even more time whenever we were assigned an essay. I suppose I could have gotten by with less, but I was determined to create some sort of identity for myself. We'd have one of those "complete this sentence" exercises, and I'd fool with the thing for hours, invariably settling on something like "A quick run around the lake? I'd love to! Just give me a moment while I strap on my wooden leg." The teacher, through word and action, conveyed the message that if this was my idea of an identity, she wanted nothing to do with it.

My fear and discomfort crept beyond the borders of the classroom and accompanied me out on to the wide boulevards. Stopping for a coffee, asking directions, depositing money in my bank account: these things were out of the question, as they involved having to speak. Before beginning school, there'd been no shutting me up, but now I was convinced that everything I said was wrong. When the phone rang, I ignored it. If someone asked me a question, I pretended to be deaf. I knew my fear was getting the best of me when I started wondering why they don't sell cuts of meat in vending machines.

My only comfort was the knowledge that I was not alone. Huddled in the hallways and making the most of our pathetic French, my fellow students and I engaged in the sort of conversation commonly overheard in refugee camps.

"Sometime me cry alone at night."

"That be common for I, also, but be more strong, you. Much work and someday you talk pretty. People start love you soon. Maybe tomorrow, okay."

Unlike the French class I had taken in New York, here there was no sense of competition. When the teacher poked a shy Korean in the eyelid with a freshly sharpened pencil, we took no comfort in the fact that, unlike Hyeyoon Cho, we all knew the irregular past tense of the verb *to defeat*. In all fairness, the teacher hadn't meant to stab the girl, but neither did she spend much time apologizing, saying only, "Well, you should have been *vkkdyo* more *kdeynfulh*."

Over time it became impossible to believe that any of us would ever improve. Fall arrived and it rained every day, meaning we would now be scolded for the water dripping from our coats and umbrellas. It was mid-October when the teacher singled me out, saying, "Every day spent with you is like having a cesarean section." And it struck me that, for the first time since arriving in France, I could understand every word that someone was saying.

Understanding doesn't mean that you can suddenly speak the language. Far from it. It's a small step, nothing more, yet its rewards are intoxicating and deceptive. The teacher continued her diatribe and I settled back, bathing in the subtle beauty of each new curse and insult.

"You exhaust me with your foolishness and reward my efforts with nothing but pain, do you understand me?"

The world opened up, and it was with great joy that I responded, "I know the thing that you speak exact now. Talk me more, you, plus, please, plus."

Jesus Shaves

"And what does one do on the fourteenth of July? Does one celebrate Bastille Day?"

It was my second month of French class, and the teacher was leading us in an exercise designed to promote the use of *one*, our latest personal pronoun.

"Might one sing on Bastille Day?" she asked. "Might one dance in the streets? Somebody give me an answer."

Printed in our textbooks was a list of major holidays accompanied by a scattered arrangement of photographs depicting French people in the act of celebration. The object of the lesson was to match the holiday with the corresponding picture. It was simple enough but seemed an exercise better suited to the use of the pronoun *they*. I didn't know about the rest

of the class, but when Bastille Day eventually rolled around, I
planned to stay home and clean my oven.

Normally, when working from the book, it was my habit
to tune out my fellow students and scout ahead, concentrating
on the question I'd calculated might fall to me, but this afternoon we were veering from the usual format. Questions were
answered on a volunteer basis, and I was able to sit back and
relax, confident that the same few students would do most
of the talking. Today's discussion was dominated by an Italian
nanny, two chatty Poles, and a pouty, plump Moroccan woman
who had grown up speaking French and had enrolled in
the class hoping to improve her spelling. She'd covered these
lessons back in the third grade and took every opportunity to
demonstrate her superiority. A question would be asked, and
she'd race to give the answer, behaving as though this were a
game show and, if quick enough, she might go home with a
tropical vacation or a side-by-side refrigerator/freezer. A trans-
fer student, by the end of her first day she'd raised her hand
so many times that her shoulder had given out. Now she just
leaned back and shouted out the answers, her bronzed arms
folded across her chest like some great grammar genie.

We'd finished discussing Bastille Day, and the teacher had
moved on to Easter, which was represented in our textbooks
by a black-and-white photograph of a chocolate bell lying
upon a bed of palm fronds.

"And what does one do on Easter? Would anyone like to
tell us?"

It was, for me, another of those holidays I'd just as soon avoid. As a rule, my family had always ignored the Easter celebrated by our non-Orthodox friends and neighbors. While the others feasted on their chocolate figurines, my brother, sisters, and I had endured epic fasts, folding our bony fingers in prayer and begging for an end to the monotony that was the Holy Trinity Church. As Greeks, we had our own Easter, which was usually observed anywhere from two to four weeks after what was known in our circle as "the American version." The reason has to do with the moon or the Orthodox calendar — something mysterious like that — though our mother always suspected it was scheduled at a later date so that the Greeks could buy their marshmallow chicks and plastic grass at drastically reduced sale prices. "The cheap sons of bitches," she'd say. "If they had their way, we'd be celebrating Christmas in the middle of goddamn February."

Because our mother was raised a Protestant, our Easters were a hybrid of the Greek and the American traditions. We received baskets of candy until we grew older and the Easter Bunny branched out. Those who smoked would awaken to find a carton of cigarettes and an assortment of disposable lighters, while the others would receive an equivalent, each according to his or her vice. In the evening we had the traditional Greek meal followed by a game in which we would toast one another with blood-colored eggs. The symbolism escapes me, but the holder of the table's one uncracked egg was supposedly rewarded with a year of good luck. I won only once. It was the year my mother died, my apartment got broken into, and I was taken to the emergency room suffering from what the attending physician diagnosed as "housewife's knee."

The Italian nanny was attempting to answer the teacher's latest question when the Moroccan student interrupted, shouting, "Excuse me, but what's an Easter?"

It would seem that despite having grown up in a Muslim country, she would have heard it mentioned once or twice, but no. "I mean it," she said. "I have no idea what you people are talking about."

The teacher called upon the rest of us to explain.

The Poles led the charge to the best of their ability. "It is," said one, "a party for the little boy of God who call his self Jesus and . . . oh, shit." She faltered and her fellow countryman came to her aid.

"He call his self Jesus and then he be die one day on two . . . morsels of . . . lumber."

The rest of the class jumped in, offering bits of information that would have given the pope an aneurysm.

"He die one day and then he go above of my head to live with your father."

"He weared of himself the long hair and after he die, the first day he come back here for to say hello to the peoples."

"He nice, the Jesus."

"He make the good things, and on the Easter we be sad because somebody makes him dead today."

Part of the problem had to do with vocabulary. Simple nouns such as *cross* and *resurrection* were beyond our grasp, let alone such complicated reflexive phrases as "to give of yourself your only begotten son." Faced with the challenge of explaining the cornerstone of Christianity, we did what any self-respecting group of people might do. We talked about food instead.

"Easter is a party for to eat of the lamb," the Italian nanny explained. "One too may eat of the chocolate."

"And who brings the chocolate?" the teacher asked.

I knew the word, so I raised my hand, saying, "The rabbit of Easter. He bring of the chocolate."

"A rabbit?" The teacher, assuming I'd used the wrong word, positioned her index fingers on top of her head, wriggling them as though they were ears. "You mean one of these? A *rabbit* rabbit?"

"Well, sure," I said. "He come in the night when one sleep on a bed. With a hand he have a basket and foods."

The teacher sighed and shook her head. As far as she was concerned, I had just explained everything that was wrong with my country. "No, no," she said. "Here in France the chocolate is brought by a big bell that flies in from Rome."

I called for a time-out. "But how do the bell know where you live?"

"Well," she said, "how does a rabbit?"

It was a decent point, but at least a rabbit has eyes. That's a start. Rabbits move from place to place, while most bells can only go back and forth — and they can't even do that on their own power. On top of that, the Easter Bunny has character. He's someone you'd like to meet and shake hands with.

A bell has all the personality of a cast-iron skillet. It's like saying that come Christmas, a magic dustpan flies in from the
North Pole, led by eight flying cinder blocks. Who wants to
stay up all night so they can see a bell? And why fly one in
from Rome when they've got more bells than they know
what to do with right here in Paris? That's the most implausi-
ble aspect of the whole story, as there's no way the bells of
France would allow a foreign worker to fly in and take their
jobs. That Roman bell would be lucky to get work cleaning
up after a French bell's dog — and even then he'd need papers. It just didn't add up.

Nothing we said was of any help to the Moroccan student. A dead man with long hair supposedly living with her
father, a leg of lamb served with palm fronds and chocolate;
equally confused and disgusted, she shrugged her massive
shoulders and turned her attention back to the comic book
she kept hidden beneath her binder.

I wondered then if, without the language barrier, my
classmates and I could have done a better job making sense of
Christianity, an idea that sounds pretty far-fetched to begin
with.

In communicating any religious belief, the operative word
is *faith,* a concept illustrated by our very presence in that classroom. Why bother struggling with the grammar lessons of a
six-year-old if each of us didn't believe that, against all reason,
we might eventually improve? If I could hope to one day carry
on a fluent conversation, it was a relatively short leap to believing that a rabbit might visit my home in the middle of the

night, leaving behind a handful of chocolate kisses and a carton of menthol cigarettes. So why stop there? If I could believe in myself, why not give other improbabilities the benefit of the doubt? I told myself that despite her past behavior, my teacher was a kind and loving person who had only my best interests at heart. I accepted the idea that an omniscient God had cast me in his own image and that he watched over me and guided me from one place to the next. The Virgin Birth, the Resurrection, and the countless miracles — my heart expanded to encompass all the wonders and possibilities of the universe.

A bell, though — that's fucked up.

The Tapeworm Is In

"WHAT DO YOU WANT to do, my friends? Go out?"

"Go out where? Go out to the discotheque?"

"No, go out to a restaurant, to the House of Butterfly."

"The House of Butterfly! Is that a pleasant restaurant?"

"It is not expensive, if that is what you mean."

"Oh, good. The matter is settled. Let us all proceed to the House of Butterfly!"

Before leaving New York, I enrolled in a monthlong French class taught by a beautiful young Parisian woman who had us memorize a series of dialogues from an audiocassette that accompanied our textbook. Because it was a beginners' course, the characters on our tape generally steered clear of slang and controversy. Avoiding both the past and the future, they embraced the moment with a stoicism common to Buddhists and recently recovered alcoholics. Fabienne, Carmen, and Eric spent a great deal of time in outdoor restaurants, discussing their love of life and enjoying colas served without ice. Passing acquaintances were introduced at regular intervals, and it was often noted that the sky was blue.

Taken one by one, the assorted nouns and verbs were within my grasp, but due to drug use and a close working relationship with chemical solvents, it was all I could do to recite my zip code, let alone an entire conversation devoted to the pleasures of direct sunlight. Hoping it might help with my memorization assignments, I broke down and bought a Walkman — which surprised me. I'd always ranked them between boa constrictors and Planet Hollywood T-shirts in terms of vulgar accessories, but once I stuck the headphones in my ears, I found I kind of liked it. The good news is that, as with a boa constrictor or a Planet Hollywood T-shirt, normal people tend to keep their distance when you're wearing a Walkman. The outside world suddenly becomes as private as you want it to be. It's like being deaf but with none of the disadvantages.

Left alone and forced to guess what everyone was screaming about, I found that walking through New York became a real pleasure. Crossing Fourteenth Street, an unmedicated psychotic would brandish a toilet brush, his mouth moving wordlessly as, in my head, the young people of France requested a table with a view of the fountain. The tape made me eager for our move to Paris, where, if nothing else, I'd be able to rattle from memory such phrases as "Let me give you my telephone number" and "I too love the sandwich."

As it turns out, I have not had occasion to use either of these sentences. Though I could invite someone to call me, the only phone number I know by heart is Eric's, the young man on my French tape. My brain is big enough to hold only one ten-digit number, and since his was there first, I have no idea how anyone might go about phoning me. I guess I could stick with the line about the sandwich, but it hardly qualifies as newsworthy. Part of the problem is that I have no one to talk to except for the members of my current French class, who mean well but exhaust me with their enthusiasm. As young and optimistic as the characters on my cassette tape, they'll occasionally invite me to join them for an after-school get-together at a nearby café. I tried it a few times but, surrounded by their fresh and smiling faces, I couldn't help but feel I'd been wrongly cast in an international Pepsi commercial. I'm just too old and worn-out to share their excitement over such innocent pleasures as a boat ride down the Seine or a potluck picnic at the base of the Eiffel Tower. It would have been good for me to get out, but when the time came, I just couldn't bring myself to attend. Neither can I manage to talk with the many strangers who automatically seek me out whenever they need a cigarette or directions to the nearest Métro station. My present French class involves no dialogue memorization, but still I find myself wearing the Walkman, mainly as a form of protection.

No great collector of music, I started off my life in Paris by listening to American books on tape. I'd never been a big fan of the medium but welcomed them as an opportunity to bone up on my English. Often these were books I would never have sat down and read. Still, though, even when they were dull I enjoyed the disconcerting combination of French life and English narration. Here was Paris, wrongly dubbed for my listening pleasure. The grand department store felt significantly less intimidating when listening to *Dolly: My Life and Other Unfinished Business*, a memoir in which the busty author describes a childhood spent picking ticks out of her grandmother's scalp. Sitting by the playground in the Luxembourg Gardens, I listened to *Lolita*, abridged with James Mason and unabridged with Jeremy Irons. There were, I noticed, half a dozen other pasty, middle-aged men who liked to gather around the monkey bars, and together we formed a small but decidedly creepy community.

Merle Haggard's *My House of Memories*, the diaries of Alan Bennett, *Treasure Island:* If a person who constantly reads is labeled a bookworm, then I was quickly becoming what might be called a tapeworm. The trouble was that I'd moved to Paris completely unprepared for my new pastime. The few tapes I owned had all been given to me at one point or another and thrown into my suitcase at the last minute. There are only so many times a grown man can listen to *The Wind in the Willows*, so I was eventually forced to consider the many French tapes given as subtle hints by our neighbors back in Normandy.

I tried listening to *The Misanthrope* and *Fontaine's Fables,* but they were just too dense for me. I'm much too lazy to make that sort of effort. Besides, if I wanted to hear people speaking wall-to-wall French, all I had to do was remove my headphones and participate in what is known as "real life," a concept as uninviting as a shampoo cocktail.

Desperate for material, I was on the verge of buying a series of Learn to Speak English tapes when my sister Amy sent a package containing several cans of clams, a sack of grits, an audio walking tour of Paris, and my very own copy of *Pocket Medical French,* a palm-size phrase book and corresponding cassette designed for doctors and nurses unfamiliar with the language. The walking tour guides one through the city's various landmarks, reciting bits of information the listener might find enlightening. I learned, for example, that in the late 1500s my little neighborhood square was a popular spot for burning people alive. Now lined with a row of small shops, the tradition continues, though in a figurative rather than literal sense.

I followed my walking tour to Notre Dame, where, bored with a lecture on the history of the flying buttress, I switched tapes and came to see Paris through the jaundiced eyes of the pocket medical guide. Spoken in English and then repeated, slowly and without emotion, in French, the phrases are short enough that I was quickly able to learn such sparkling conversational icebreakers as "Remove your dentures and all of your jewelry" and "You now need to deliver the afterbirth." Though I have yet to use any of my new commands and questions, I find that, in learning them, I am finally able to imagine myself Walkman-free and plunging headfirst into an active and rewarding social life. That's me at the glittering party, re-filling my champagne glass and turning to ask my host if he's noticed any unusual discharge. "We need to start an IV," I'll say to the countess while boarding her yacht. "But first could I trouble you for a stool sample?"

With practice I will eventually realize my goal; in the meantime, come to Paris and you will find me, headphones plugged tight in my external audio meatus, walking the quays and whispering, "Has anything else been inserted into your anus? Has anything else been inserted into your anus?"

Make That a Double

THERE ARE, I HAVE NOTICED, two basic types of French spoken by Americans vacationing in Paris: the Hard Kind and the Easy Kind. The Hard Kind involves the conjugation of wily verbs and the science of placing them alongside various other words in order to form such sentences as "I go him say good afternoon" and "No, not to him I no go it him say now."

The second, less complicated form of French amounts to screaming English at the top of your lungs, much the same way you'd shout at a deaf person or the dog you thought you could train to stay off the sofa. Doubt and hesitation are completely unnecessary, as Easy French is rooted in the premise that, if properly packed, the rest of the world could fit within the confines of Reno, Nevada. The speaker carries no pocket dictionary and never suffers the humiliation that inevitably comes with pointing to the menu and ordering the day of the week. With Easy French, eating out involves a simple "BRING ME A STEAK."

Having undertaken the study of Hard French, I'll overhear such requests and glare across the room, thinking, "That's *Mister* Steak to you, buddy." Of all the stumbling blocks inherent in learning this language, the greatest for me is the principle that each noun has a corresponding sex that affects both its articles and its adjectives. Because it is a female and lays eggs, a chicken is masculine. *Vagina* is masculine as well, while the word *masculinity* is feminine. Forced by the grammar to take a stand one way or the other, *hermaphrodite* is male and *indecisiveness* female.

I spent months searching for some secret code before I realized that common sense has nothing to do with it. *Hysteria, psychosis, torture, depression:* I was told that if something is unpleasant, it's probably feminine. This encouraged me, but the theory was blown by such masculine nouns as *murder, toothache,* and *Rollerblade.* I have no problem learning the words themselves, it's the sexes that trip me up and refuse to stick.

What's the trick to remembering that a sandwich is masculine? What qualities does it share with anyone in possession of a penis? I'll tell myself that a sandwich is masculine because if left alone for a week or two, it will eventually grow a beard. This works until it's time to order and I decide that because it sometimes loses its makeup, a sandwich is undoubtedly feminine.

I just can't manage to keep my stories straight. Hoping I might learn through repetition, I tried using gender in my everyday English. "Hi, guys," I'd say, opening a new box of paper clips, or "Hey, Hugh, have you seen my belt? I can't find her anywhere." I invented personalities for the objects on my dresser and set them up on blind dates. When things didn't work out with my wallet, my watch drove a wedge between my hairbrush and my lighter. The scenarios reminded me of my youth, when my sisters and I would enact epic dramas with our food. Ketchup-wigged french fries would march across our plates, engaging in brief affairs or heated disputes over carrot coins while burly chicken legs guarded the perimeter, ready to jump in should things get out of hand. Sexes were assigned at our discretion and were subject to change from one night to the next — unlike here, where the corncob and the string bean remain locked in their rigid masculine roles. Say what you like about southern social structure, but at least in North Carolina a hot dog is free to swing both ways.

Nothing in France is free from sexual assignment. I was leafing through the dictionary, trying to complete a homework assignment, when I noticed the French had prescribed genders for the various land masses and natural wonders we Americans had always thought of as sexless, Niagara Falls is feminine and, against all reason, the Grand Canyon is masculine. Georgia and Florida are female, but Montana and Utah are male. New England is a she, while the vast area we call the Midwest is just one big guy. I wonder whose job it was to assign these sexes in the first place. Did he do his work right there in the sanitarium, or did they rent him a little office where he could get away from all the noise?

There are times when you can swallow the article and others when it must be clearly pronounced, as the word has two different meanings, one masculine and the other feminine. It should be fairly obvious that I cooked an omelette in a frying pan rather than in a wood stove, but it bothers me to make the same mistakes over and over again. I wind up exhausting the listener before I even get to the verb.

My confidence hit a new low when my friend Adeline told me that French children often make mistakes, but never with the sex of their nouns. "It's just something we grow up with," she said. "We hear the gender once, and then think of it as part of the word. There's nothing to it."

It's a pretty grim world when I can't even feel superior to a toddler. Tired of embarrassing myself in front of two-year-olds, I've started referring to everything in the plural, which can get expensive but has solved a lot of my problems. In saying *a melon*, you need to use the masculine article. In saying *the melons*, you use the plural article, which does not reflect gender and is the same for both the masculine and the feminine. Ask for two or ten or three hundred melons, and the number lets you off the hook by replacing the article altogether. A masculine kilo of feminine tomatoes presents a sexual problem easily solved by asking for two kilos of tomatoes. I've started using the plural while shopping, and Hugh has started using it in our cramped kitchen, where he stands huddled in the corner, shouting, "What do we need with four pounds of tomatoes?"

I answer that I'm sure we can use them for something. The only hard part is finding someplace to put them. They won't fit in the refrigerator, as I filled the last remaining shelf with the two chickens I bought from the butcher the night before, forgetting that we were still working our way through a pair of pork roasts the size of Duraflame logs. "We could put them next to the radios," I say, "or grind them for sauce in one of the blenders. Don't get so mad. Having four pounds of tomatoes is better than having no tomatoes at all, isn't it?"

Hugh tells me that the market is off-limits until my French improves. He's pretty steamed, but I think he'll get over it when he sees the CD players I got him for his birthday.

Remembering My Childhood
on the Continent of Africa

WHEN HUGH WAS IN THE FIFTH GRADE, his class took a field trip to an Ethiopian slaughterhouse. He was living in Addis Ababa at the time, and the slaughterhouse was chosen because, he says, "it was convenient."

This was a school system in which the matter of proximity outweighed such petty concerns as what may or may not be appropriate for a busload of eleven-year-olds. "What?" I asked. "Were there no autopsies scheduled at the local morgue? Was the federal prison just a bit too far out of the way?"

Hugh defends his former school, saying, "Well, isn't that the whole point of a field trip? To see something new?"

"Technically yes, but . . ."

"All right then," he says. "So we saw some new things."

One of his field trips was literally a trip to a field where the class watched a wrinkled man fill his mouth with rotten goat meat and feed it to a pack of waiting hyenas. On another occasion they were taken to examine the bloodied bedroom curtains hanging in the palace of the former dictator. There were tamer trips, to textile factories and sugar refineries, but my favorite is always the slaughterhouse. It wasn't a big company, just a small rural enterprise run by a couple of brothers operating out of a low-ceilinged concrete building. Following a brief lecture on the importance of proper sanitation, a small white piglet was herded into the room, its dainty hooves clicking against the concrete floor. The class gathered in a circle to get a better look at the animal, who seemed delighted with the attention he was getting. He turned from face to face and was looking up at Hugh when one of the brothers drew a pistol from his back pocket, held it against the animal's temple, and shot the piglet, execution-style. Blood spattered, frightened children wept, and the man with the gun offered the teacher and bus driver some meat from a freshly slaughtered goat.

When I'm told such stories, it's all I can do to hold back my feelings of jealousy. An Ethiopian slaughterhouse. Some people have all the luck. When I was in elementary school, the best we ever got was a trip to Old Salem or Colonial Williamsburg, one of those preserved brick villages where time supposedly stands still and someone earns his living as a town crier. There was always a blacksmith, a group of wandering patriots, and a collection of bonneted women hawking corn bread or gingersnaps made "the ol'-fashioned way."

Every now and then you might come across a doer of bad deeds serving time in the stocks, but that was generally as exciting as it got.

Certain events are parallel, but compared with Hugh's, my childhood was unspeakably dull. When I was seven years old, my family moved to North Carolina. When he was seven years old, Hugh's family moved to the Congo. We had a collie and a house cat. They had a monkey and two horses named Charlie Brown and Satan. I threw stones at stop signs. Hugh threw stones at crocodiles. The verbs are the same, but he definitely wins the prize when it comes to nouns and objects. An eventful day for my mother might have involved a trip to the dry cleaner or a conversation with the potato-chip deliveryman. Asked one ordinary Congo afternoon what she'd done with her day, Hugh's mother answered that she and a fellow member of the Ladies' Club had visited a leper colony on the outskirts of Kinshasa. No reason was given for the expedition, though chances are she was staking it out for a future field trip.

Due to his upbringing, Hugh sits through inane movies never realizing that they're often based on inane television shows. There were no poker-faced sitcom martians in his part of Africa, no oil-rich hillbillies or aproned brides trying to wean themselves from the practice of witchcraft. From time to time a movie would arrive packed in a dented canister, the film scratched and faded from its slow trip around the world. The theater consisted of a few dozen folding chairs arranged before a bedsheet or the blank wall of a vacant hangar out near the airstrip. Occasionally a man would sell warm soft drinks out of a cardboard box, but that was it in terms of concessions.

When I was young, I went to the theater at the nearby shopping center and watched a movie about a talking Volkswagen. I believe the little car had a taste for mischief but I can't be certain, as both the movie and the afternoon proved unremarkable and have faded from my memory. Hugh saw the same movie a few years after it was released. His family had left the Congo by this time and were living in Ethiopia. Like me, Hugh saw the movie by himself on a weekend afternoon. Unlike me, he left the theater two hours later, to find a dead man hanging from a telephone pole at the far end of the unpaved parking lot. None of the people who'd seen the movie seemed to care about the dead man. They stared at him for a moment or two and then headed home, saying they'd never seen anything as crazy as that talking Volkswagen. His father was late picking him up, so Hugh just stood there for an hour, watching the dead man dangle and turn in the breeze. The death was not reported in the newspaper, and when Hugh related the story to his friends, they said, "You saw the movie about the talking car?"

I could have done without the flies and the primitive theaters, but I wouldn't have minded growing up with a houseful of servants. In North Carolina it wasn't unusual to have a once-a-week maid, but Hugh's family had houseboys, a word that never fails to charge my imagination. They had cooks and drivers, and guards who occupied a gatehouse, armed with machetes. Seeing as I had regularly petitioned my parents for an electric fence, the business with the guards strikes me as the last word in quiet sophistication. Having protection suggests that you are important. Having that protection paid for by the government is even better, as it suggests your safety is of interest to someone other than yourself.

Hugh's father was a career officer with the U.S. State Department, and every morning a black sedan carried him off to the embassy. I'm told it's not as glamorous as it sounds, but in terms of fun for the entire family, I'm fairly confident that it beats the sack race at the annual IBM picnic. By the age of three, Hugh was already carrying a diplomatic passport. The rules that applied to others did not apply to him. No tickets, no arrests, no luggage search: he was officially licensed to act like a brat. Being an American, it was expected of him, and who was he to deny the world an occasional tantrum?

They weren't rich, but what Hugh's family lacked financially they more than made up for with the sort of exoticism that works wonders at cocktail parties, leading always to the remark "That sounds fascinating." It's a compliment one rarely receives when describing an adolescence spent drinking Slush Puppies at the North Hills Mall. No fifteen-foot python ever wandered on to my school's basketball court. I begged, I prayed nightly, but it just never happened. Neither did I get to witness a military coup in which forces sympathetic to the colonel arrived late at night to assassinate my next-door neighbor. Hugh had been at the Addis Ababa teen club when the electricity was cut off and soldiers arrived to evacuate the building. He and his friends had to hide in the back of a jeep and cover themselves with blankets during the ride home. It's something that sticks in his mind for one reason or another.

Among my personal highlights is the memory of having my picture taken with Uncle Paul, the officially blind host of a Raleigh children's television show. Among Hugh's is the memory of having his picture taken with Buzz Aldrin on the last leg of the astronaut's world tour. The man who had walked on the moon placed his hand on Hugh's shoulder and offered to sign his autograph book. The man who led Wake County schoolchildren in afternoon song turned at the sound of my voice and asked, "So what's your name, princess?"

When I was fourteen years old, I was sent to spend ten days with my maternal grandmother in western New York State. She was a small and private woman named Billie, and though she never came right out and asked, I had the distinct impression she had no idea who I was. It was the way she looked at me, squinting through her glasses while chewing on her lower lip. That, coupled with the fact that she never once called me by name. "Oh," she'd say, "are you still here?" She was just beginning her long struggle with Alzheimer's disease, and each time I entered the room, I felt the need to reintroduce myself and set her at ease. "Hi, it's me. Sharon's boy, David. I was just in the kitchen admiring your collection of ceramic toads." Aside from a few trips to summer camp, this was the longest I'd ever been away from home, and I like to think I was toughened by the experience.

About the same time I was frightening my grandmother, Hugh and his family were packing their belongings for a move to Somalia. There were no English-speaking schools in Mogadishu, so, after a few months spent lying around the family compound with his pet monkey, Hugh was sent back to Ethiopia to live with a beer enthusiast his father had met at a cocktail party. Mr. Hoyt installed security systems in foreign embassies. He and his family gave Hugh a room. They invited him to join them at the table, but that was as far as they extended themselves. No one ever asked him when his birthday was, so when the day came, he kept it to himself. There was no telephone service between Ethiopia and Somalia, and letters to his parents were sent to Washington and then forwarded on to Mogadishu, meaning that his news was more than a month old by the time they got it. I suppose it wasn't much different than living as a foreign-exchange student. Young people do it all the time, but to me it sounds awful. The Hoyts had two sons about Hugh's age who were always saying things like "Hey that's *our* sofa you're sitting on" and "Hands off that ornamental stein. It doesn't belong to you."

He'd been living with these people for a year when he overheard Mr. Hoyt tell a friend that he and his family would soon be moving to Munich, Germany, the beer capital of the world.

"And that worried me," Hugh said, "because it meant I'd have to find some other place to live."

Where I come from, finding shelter is a problem the average teenager might confidently leave to his parents. It was just something that came with having a mom and a dad. Worried that he might be sent to live with his grandparents in Kentucky, Hugh turned to the school's guidance counselor, who knew of a family whose son had recently left for college. And so he spent another year living with strangers and not mentioning his birthday. While I wouldn't have wanted to do it myself, I can't help but envy the sense of fortitude he gained from the experience. After graduating from college, he moved to France knowing only the phrase "Do you speak French?" — a question guaranteed to get you nowhere unless you also speak the language.

While living in Africa, Hugh and his family took frequent vacations, often in the company of their monkey. The Nairobi Hilton, some suite of high-ceilinged rooms in Cairo or Khartoum: these are the places his people recall when gathered at a common table. "Was that the summer we spent in Beirut or, no, I'm thinking of the time we sailed from Cyprus and took the *Orient Express* to Istanbul."

Theirs was the life I dreamt about during my vacations in eastern North Carolina. Hugh's family was hobnobbing with chiefs and sultans while I ate hush puppies at the Sanitary Fish Market in Morehead City, a beach towel wrapped like a hijab around my head. Someone unknown to me was very likely standing in a muddy ditch and dreaming of an evening spent sitting in a clean family restaurant, drinking iced tea and working his way through an extra-large seaman's platter, but that did not concern me, as it meant I should have been happy with what I had. Rather than surrender to my bitterness, I have learned to take satisfaction in the life that Hugh has led. His stories have, over time, become my own. I say this with no trace of a kumbaya. There is no spiritual symbiosis; I'm just a petty thief who lifts his memories the same way I'll take a handful of change left on his dresser. When my own experiences fall short of the mark, I just go out and spend some of his. It is with pleasure that I sometimes recall the dead man's purpled face or the report of the handgun ringing in my ears as I studied the blood pooling beneath the dead white piglet. On the way back from the slaughterhouse, we stopped for Cokes in the village of Mojo, where the gas-station owner had arranged a few tables and chairs beneath a dying canopy of vines. It was late afternoon by the time we returned to school, where a second bus carried me to the foot of Coffeeboard Road. Once there, I walked through a grove of eucalyptus trees and alongside a bald pasture of starving cattle, past the guard napping in his gatehouse, and into the waiting arms of my monkey.

21 Down

WHEN ASKED "What do we need to learn this for?" any high-school teacher can confidently answer that, regardless of the subject, the knowledge will come in handy once the student hits middle age and starts working crossword puzzles in order to stave off the terrible loneliness. Because it's true. Latin, geography, the gods of ancient Greece and Rome: unless you know these things, you'll be limited to doing the puzzles in *People* magazine, where the clues read "Movie title, *Gone* _____ *the Wind*" and "It holds up your pants." It's not such a terrible place to start, but the joy of accomplishment wears off fairly quickly.

I've been told that crosswords puzzles help fight the advance of Alzheimer's Disease, but that had nothing to do with my initiation. I started working them a few years ago, after dropping by to visit a former boyfriend. The man was and still is exceedingly — almost painfully — handsome. In Eugene Maleska crossword terminology, he's braw and pulchritudinous, while Will Shortz, current puzzle editor for *The New York Times*, might define him as a "wower," the clue being "Turns heads, in a way."

Because my former boyfriend was so good-looking, I had always insisted that he must also be stupid, the reason being that it was simply unfair for someone to be blessed with both chiseled features and basic conversational skills. He was, of course, much smarter than I gave him credit for, and he eventually proved his intelligence by breaking up with me. We both wound up moving to New York, where over time we developed what currently passes for a casual friendship. I stopped by his office one afternoon, hoping that maybe he'd lost a few teeth, and there he was, leaning back in his chair and finishing the Friday *New York Times* puzzle with a ballpoint pen. The capital city of Tuvalu, a long-forgotten Olympic weight lifter, a fifteen-letter word for *dervish:* "Oh, that," he said. "It's just something I do with my hands while I'm on the phone."

I was devastated.

The *New York Times* puzzles grow progressively harder as the week advances, with Monday being the easiest and Saturday requiring the sort of mind that can bend spoons. It took me several days to complete my first Monday puzzle, and after I'd finished, I carried it around in my wallet, hoping that someone might stop me on the street and ask to see it. "No!"

I imagined the speaker saying, "You mean to say you're only forty years old and you completed this puzzle all by yourself? Why, that's practically unheard-of!"

It's taken me two years to advance to the level of a Thursday, but still my seven hours of work can be undone by a single question pertaining to sports or opera. Since moving to France my hobby has gotten considerably more expensive. The time difference isn't winning me any friends, either. "Jesus Christ," my father will say. "It's four o'clock in the morning. Who cares who won the 'sixty-four U.S. Open?" The overseas calls were killing me, so I invested in an atlas and a shelfful of almanacs and reference books. I don't always find what I'm looking for, but in searching for an answer, I'll often come across bits of information I can use in some later puzzle. The Indian emperors of the Kanva dynasty, Ted Bundy's assumed name, the winners of the 1974 Tony Awards: these things are bound to come in handy eventually.

The *New York Times* puzzle is printed in the *International Herald Tribune,* a paper sold at just about any Paris newsstand. I was recently attempting to finish a Wednesday and, stumped over 21 down, "A friend of Job," I turned to something called *The Order of Things.* It's a reference book given to me by my sister Amy, and it's full of useful information. While thumbing toward the Bible section, I came across a list of phobias arranged into various classifications. I found myself delighted by genuphobia (the fear of knees), pogonophobia (fear of beards), and keraunothnetophobia (the nineteen-letter word used to identify those who fear the fall of man-made satellites). Reading over the lists, I found myself trying to imagine the support groups for those struggling to overcome their fears of rust or teeth, heredity or string. There would definitely be daytime meetings for the achluophobics (who fear nightfall), and evening get-togethers for the daylight-fearing phengophobics. Those who fear crowds would have to meet one-on-one, and those who fear psychiatry would be forced to find comfort in untrained friends and family members.

The long list of situational phobias includes the fears of being bound, beaten, locked into an enclosed area, and smeared with human waste. Their inclusion mystifies me, as it suggests that these fears might be considered in any way unreasonable. I asked myself, *Who wants to be handcuffed and covered in human feces?* And then, without even opening my address book, I thought of three people right off the bat. This frightened me, but apparently it's my own private phobia. I found no listing for those who fear they know too many masochists. Neither did I find an entry for those who fear the terrible truth that their self-worth is based entirely on the completion of a daily crossword puzzle. Because I can't seem to find it anywhere, I'm guaranteed that such a word actually exists. It will undoubtedly pop up in some future puzzle, the clue being "You, honestly."

The City of Light
in the Dark

When asked to account for the time I've spent in Paris, I reach for my carton of ticket stubs and groan beneath its weight. I've been here for more than a year, and while I haven't seen the Louvre or the Pantheon, I have seen *The Alamo* and *The Bridge on the River Kwai*. I haven't made it to Versailles but did manage to catch *Oklahoma!*, *Brazil*, and *Nashville*. Aside from an occasional trip to the flea market, my knowledge of Paris is limited to what I learned in *Gigi*.

When visitors come from the United States, I draw up little itineraries. "If we go to the three o'clock *Operation Petticoat*, that should give us enough time to make it across town for the six o'clock screening of *It Is Necessary to Save the Soldier Ryan*, unless, of course, you'd rather see the four o'clock

Ruggles of Red Gap and the seven o'clock *Roman Holiday*. Me, I'm pretty flexible, so why don't *you* decide."

My guests' decisions prove that I am a poor judge of my own character. Ayatollahs are flexible. I am not. Given the choice between four perfectly acceptable movies, they invariably opt for a walk through the Picasso museum or a tour of the cathedral, saying, "I didn't come all the way to Paris so I can sit in the dark."

They make it sound so bad. "Yes," I say, "but this is the French dark. It's . . . darker than the dark we have back home." In the end I give them a map and spare set of keys. They see Notre Dame, I see *The Hunchback of Notre Dame*.

I'm often told that it's wasteful to live in Paris and spend all my time watching American movies, that it's like going to Cairo to eat cheeseburgers. "You could do that back home," people say. But they're wrong. I couldn't live like this in the United States. With very few exceptions, video killed the American revival house. If you want to see a Boris Karloff movie, you have to rent it and watch it on a television set. In Paris it costs as much to rent a movie as it does to go to the theater. French people enjoy going out and watching their movies on a big screen. On any given week one has at least 250 pictures to choose from, at least a third of them in English. There are all the recent American releases, along with any old movie you'd ever want to see. On Easter, having learned that *The Greatest Story Ever Told* was sold out, I just crossed the street and saw *Superfly*, the second-greatest story ever told. Unless they're for children, all movies are shown in their original English with French subtitles. Someone might say, "Get your fat ass out of here before I do something I regret," and the screen will read, "Leave."

I sometimes wonder why I even bothered with French class. "I am truly delighted to make your acquaintance," "I heartily thank you for this succulent meal" — I have yet to use either of these pleasantries. Since moving to Paris my most often used phrase is "One place, please." That's what one says at the box office when ordering a ticket, and I say it quite well. In New York I'd go to the movies three or four times a week. Here I've upped it to six or seven, mainly because I'm too lazy to do anything else. Fortunately, going to the movies seems to suddenly qualify as an intellectual accomplishment, on a par with reading a book or devoting time to serious thought. It's not that the movies have gotten any more strenuous, it's just that a lot of people are as lazy as I am, and together we've agreed to lower the bar.

Circumstances foster my laziness. Within a five-block radius of my apartment there are four first-run multiplexes and a dozen thirty-to-fifty-seat revival houses with rotating programs devoted to obscure and well-known actors, directors, and genres. These are the mom-and-pop theaters, willing to proceed with the two o'clock showing of *The Honeymoon Killers* even if I'm the only one in the house. It's as if someone had outfitted his den with a big screen and comfortable chairs. The woman at the box office sells you a ticket, rips it in half, and hands you the stub. Inside the theater you're warmly greeted by a hostess who examines your stub and tears it just enough to make her presence felt. Somewhere along the line someone decided that this activity is worthy of a tip, so you give the woman some change, though I've never known why. It's a mystery, like those big heads on Easter Island or the popularity of the teeny-weeny knapsack.

I'm so grateful such theaters still exist that I'd gladly tip the projectionist as well. Like the restaurants with only three tables, I wonder how some of these places manage to stay open. In America the theaters make most of their money at the concession stand, but here, at least in the smaller places, you'll find nothing but an ice-cream machine tucked away between the bathroom and the fire exit. The larger theaters offer a bit more, but it's still mainly candy and ice cream sold by a vendor with a tray around his neck. American theaters have begun issuing enormous cardboard trays, and it's only a matter of time before the marquees read TRY OUR BARBECUED RIBS! or COMPLIMENTARY BAKED POTATO WITH EVERY THIRTY-TWO-OUNCE SIRLOIN. When they started selling nachos, I knew that chicken wings couldn't be far behind. Today's hot dogs are only clearing the way for tomorrow's hamburgers, and from there it's only a short leap to the distribution of cutlery.

I've never considered myself an across-the-board apologist for the French, but there's a lot to be said for an entire population that never, under any circumstances, talks during the picture. I've sat through Saturday-night slasher movies with audiences of teenagers and even then nobody has said a word. I can't remember the last time I've enjoyed silence in an American theater. It's easy to believe that our audiences spend the day saying nothing, actually saving their voices for the moment the picture begins. At an average New York screening I once tapped the shoulder of the man in front of me, interrupting his spot review to ask if he planned on talking through the entire movie.

"Well . . . yeah. What about it?" He said this with no trace of shame or apology. It was as if I'd asked if he planned to circulate his blood or draw air into his lungs. "Gee, why wouldn't I?" I moved away from the critic and found myself sitting beside a clairvoyant who loudly predicted the fates of the various characters seen moving their lips up on the screen. Next came an elderly couple constantly convinced they were missing something. A stranger would knock on the door, and they'd ask, "Who's he?" I wanted to assure them that all their questions would be answered in due time, but I don't believe in talking during movies, so I moved again, hoping I might be lucky enough to find a seat between two people who had either fallen asleep or died.

At a theater in Chicago I once sat beside a man who watched the movie while listening to a Cubs game on his transistor radio. When the usher was called, the sports fan announced that this was a free country and that he wanted to listen to the goddamn game. "Is there a law against doing both things at once?" he asked. "Is there a law? Show me the law, and I'll turn off my radio."

Sitting in Paris and watching my American movies, I think of the man with the transistor radio and feel the exact opposite of homesick. The camera glides over the cities of my past, capturing their energetic skylines just before they're destroyed by the terrorist's bomb or advancing alien warship. New York, Chicago, San Francisco: it's like seeing pictures of people I know I could still sleep with if I wanted to. When the high-speed chases and mandatory shoot-outs become too repetitive, I head over to the revival houses and watch gentler movies in which the couples sleep in separate beds and everyone wears a hat. As my ticket is ripped I'll briefly consider all the constructive things I could be doing. I think of the parks and the restaurants, of the pleasantries I'll never use on the friends I am failing to make. I think of the great city teeming on the other side of that curtain, and then the lights go down, and I love Paris.

I Pledge Allegiance
to the Bag

ONE OF THE DRAWBACKS to living in Paris is that people often refer to you as an expatriate, occasionally shortening the word to an even more irritating "ex-pat." It is implied that anything might take you to London or Saint Kitts, but if you live in Paris, it must be because you hate the United States. What can I say? There may be bands of turncoats secretly plotting to overthrow their former government, but I certainly haven't run across them. I guess we don't shop at the same boutiques. The Americans I've befriended don't hate the United States, they simply prefer France for one reason or another. Some of them married French people or came here for work, but none of them viewed the move as a political act.

Like me, my American friends are sometimes called upon to defend their country, usually at dinner parties where everyone's had a bit too much to drink. The United States will have done something the French don't like, and people will behave as though it's all my fault. I'm always taken off guard when a hostess accuses me of unfairly taxing her beef. *Wait a minute,* I think. *Did I do that?* Whenever my government refuses to sign a treaty or decides to throw its weight around in NATO, I become not an American citizen but, rather, America itself, all fifty states and Puerto Rico sitting at the table with gravy on my chin.

During Bill Clinton's impeachment hearings, my French teacher would often single me out, saying, "You Americans, you're all such puritans." Citizens of Europe and Asia, my fellow class members would agree with her, while I'd wonder, *Are we?* I'm sure the reputation isn't entirely undeserved, but how prudish can we be when almost everyone I know has engaged in a three-way?

I'd never thought much about how Americans were viewed overseas until I came to France and was expected to look and behave in a certain way. "You're not supposed to be smoking," my classmates would tell me. "You're from the United States." Europeans expected me to regularly wash my hands with prepackaged towelettes and to automatically reject all unpasteurized dairy products. If I was thin, it must be because I'd recently lost the extra fifty pounds traditionally cushioning the standard American ass. If I was pushy, it was typical; and if I wasn't, it was probably due to Prozac.

Where did people get these ideas, and how valid are they? I asked myself these questions when, after spending nine months in France, I returned to the United States for a five-week trip to twenty cities. The plane hadn't even left Paris when the New Yorker seated beside me turned to ask how much I'd paid for my round-trip ticket. Americans are famous for talking about money, and I do everything possible to keep our reputation alive. "Guess how much I spent on your birthday present?" I ask. "Tell me, how much rent do you pay?" "What did it cost you to have that lung removed?" I horrify the French every time I open my mouth. They seem to view such questions as prying or boastful, but to me they're perfectly normal. You have to talk about something, and money seems to have filled the conversational niche made available when people stopped discussing the Constitutional Convention of 1787.

During my five weeks in the United States, I spent a lot of time on planes and waiting around in airports, where the image of Americans as hard workers was clearly up for grabs. Most passengers were in favor of the stereotype, while the majority of airport employees seemed dead set against it. Standing in long lines, I could easily see how we earned our reputation as a friendly and talkative people. Conversations tended to revolve around the incompetence of the person standing behind the cash register or computer terminal, but even when pressed for time, I found most travelers to be tolerant and good-natured, much more willing to laugh than to cause a stink. People expressed the hope that they might catch their plane, that they might leave on time, and that their luggage might eventually join them once they reached their destination. Once considered relentlessly positive, we seem to have substantially lowered our expectations.

I thought a lot about American optimism when, on a flight from Chicago to San Francisco, I watched one of those video magazines stitched together from a week's worth of soft network news reports. There was the standard "just how safe are they?" report focusing on chopsticks or cardboard boxes, followed by the latest study proving that people who wear socks to bed are likely to live five hours longer than the rest of us. Then came a human-interest story about a New York City program designed to expose the homeless to great works of art. The segment opened with a genteel woman standing before a Rembrandt painting and addressing a group of unshaven men dressed in ragged clothing. The woman lectured on the play of light and shadow. She addressed the emotions provoked by the artist's somber choice of colors, and her eyes glittered as she spoke. Interviewed later, one of the men conceded that the painting was nice, saying, "Sure, I liked it okay." Then the camera cut back to the woman, who explained that art appreciation was a form of therapy that would hopefully help get these men back on their feet. Here was an example of insane optimism coupled with the naive popular belief that a few hours of therapy can cure everything from chronic obesity to a lifetime of poverty. It's always nice to get out of the cold, but I think this woman was fooling herself in believing that these men would prefer a Rembrandt to a couple of reubens.

For all our earnest recycling, America is still seen as a ter-

ribly wasteful country. It's a stigma we've earned and are trying to overcome with our own unique blend of guilt and
hypocrisy. On the first night of my trip, while brushing my
teeth in the bathroom of my $270-a-night hotel, I noticed a
little sign reading SAVE THE PLANET!

Okay, I thought, *but how?*

The card reported the amount of water used every year
in hotel laundry rooms and suggested that, in having my
sheets and towels changed on a daily basis, I was taking this
precious water directly from the cupped hands of a dehy-
drated child. I noticed there was no similar plea encouraging
me to conserve the hot water that came with my fifteen-
dollar pot of room-service tea, but that apparently was a different kind of water. I found an identical SAVE THE PLANET
card in each of my subsequent hotel rooms, and it got on my
nerves in no time. I don't mind reusing a towel, but if they're
charging that much for a hotel, I *want* my sheets changed
every day. If I'd felt like sharing my bed with trillions of dead
skin cells, I would have stayed at home or spent the night
with friends. I was never the one paying for the room, but
still, I resent being made to feel guilty for requesting a service
an expensive hotel is generally expected to perform.

Pandas and rain forests are never mentioned when it
comes to the millions of people taking joyrides in their Range
Rovers. Rather, it's the little things we're strong-armed into
conserving. At a chain coffee bar in San Francisco, I saw a sign
near the cream counter that read NAPKINS COME FROM TREES —
CONSERVE! In case you missed the first sign, there was a second

one two feet away, reading YOU WASTE NAPKINS — YOU WASTE TREES!!! The cups, of course, are also made of paper, yet there's no mention of the mighty redwood when you order your four-dollar coffee. The guilt applies only to those things that are being given away for free. Were they to charge you ten cents per napkin, they would undoubtedly make them much thinner so you'd need to waste even more in order to fight back the piping hot geyser forever spouting from the little hole conveniently located in the lid of your cup.

Traveling across the United States, it's easy to see why Americans are often thought of as stupid. At the San Diego Zoo, right near the primate habitats, there's a display featuring half a dozen life-size gorillas made out of bronze. Posted nearby is a sign reading CAUTION: GORILLA STATUES MAY BE HOT. Everywhere you turn, the obvious is being stated. CANNON MAY BE LOUD. MOVING SIDEWALK IS ABOUT TO END. To people who don't run around suing one another, such signs suggest a crippling lack of intelligence. Place bronze statues beneath the southern California sun, and of course they're going to get hot. Cannons are supposed to be loud, that's their claim to fame, and — like it or not — the moving sidewalk is bound to end sooner or later. It's hard trying to explain a country whose motto has become You can't claim I didn't warn you. What can you say about the family who is suing the railroad after their drunk son was killed walking on the tracks? Trains don't normally sneak up on people. Unless they've derailed, you pretty much know where to find them. The young man wasn't deaf and blind. No one had tied him to the tracks, so what's there to sue about?

While at a loss to explain some things, I take great joy in explaining others. After returning from my trip, I went to my regular place to have my hair cut. They'd given me a shampoo and I was sitting with a towel on my head when Pascal, the shop owner, handed me a popular French gossip magazine featuring a story on Jodie Foster and her new baby. Pascal, who speaks English, is "aped over Jodie Foster" and owns all her movies on videotape. His dream is to frost her tips while asking behind-the-scenes questions about *Sommersby*.

"I've been looking at this one photo," he said, "but there is something here that I am not making out."

He pointed to a picture of the actress walking down a California beach with an unidentified friend who held the baby against her chest. A large dog ran just ahead of the women and splashed in the surf.

"I can see that Jodie Foster is holding in one hand a leash," Pascal said. "But what is it she is carrying in the other hand? I have asked many people, but nobody knows for sure."

I brought the magazine close to my face and studied it for a moment. "Well," I said, "she appears to be carrying a plastic bag of dog shit."

"Go out of here, you nut." He seemed almost angry. "Jodie Foster is the biggest star. She won an Academy Award two times, so why would she like to carry a bag that is full of shit? Nobody would do that but a crazy person." He called to his four employees. "Get over here and listen to what he's saying, the crazy nut."

In trying to communicate why an Academy Award–winning actress might walk down the beach carrying a plastic bag full of dog feces, I got the sort of lump in my throat that other people might get while singing their national anthem. It was the pride one can feel only when, far from home and surrounded by a captive audience, you are called upon to explain what is undoubtedly the single greatest thing about your country.

"Well," I said, "it goes like this . . ."

Picka Pocketoni

IT WAS JULY, and Hugh and I were taking the Paris Métro from our neighborhood to a store where we hoped to buy a good deal of burlap. The store was located on the other side of town, and the trip involved taking one train and then switching to another. During the summer months a great number of American vacationers can be found riding the Métro, and their voices tend to carry. It's something I hadn't noticed until leaving home, but we are a loud people. The trumpeting elephants of the human race. Questions, observations, the locations of blisters and rashes — everything is delivered as though it were an announcement.

On the first of our two trains I listened to a quartet of college-age Texans who sat beneath a sign instructing passengers to surrender their folding seats and stand should the foyer of the train become too crowded. The foyer of the train quickly became too crowded, and while the others stood to make more room, the young Texans remained seated and raised their voices in order to continue their debate, the topic being "Which is a better city, Houston or Paris?" It was a hot afternoon, and the subject of air-conditioning came into play. Houston had it, Paris did not. Houston also had ice cubes, tacos, plenty of free parking, and something called a Sonic Burger. Things were not looking good for Paris, which lost valuable points every time the train stopped to accept more passengers. The crowds packed in, surrounding the seated Texans and reducing them to four disembodied voices. From the far corner of the car, one of them shouted that they were tired and dirty and ready to catch the next plane home. The voice was weary and hopeless, and I identified completely. It was the same way I'd felt on my last visit to Houston.

Hugh and I disembarked to the strains of "Texas, Our Texas" and boarded our second train, where an American couple in their late forties stood hugging the floor-to-ceiling support pole. There's no sign saying so, but such poles are not considered private. They're put there for everyone's use. You don't treat it like a fireman's pole; rather, you grasp it with one hand and stand back at a respectable distance. It's not all that difficult to figure out, even if you come from a town without any public transportation.

The train left the station, and needing something to hold on to, I wedged my hand between the American couple and grabbed the pole at waist level. The man turned to the woman, saying, "Peeeeew, can you smell that? That is pure French, baby." He removed one of his hands from the pole and waved it back and forth in front of his face. "Yes indeed," he said. "This little froggy is ripe."

It took a moment to realize he was talking about me.

The woman wrinkled her nose. "Golly Pete!" she said, "Do they all smell this bad?"

"It's pretty typical," the man said. "I'm willing to bet that our little friend here hasn't had a bath in a good two weeks. I mean, Jesus Christ, someone should hang a deodorizer around this guy's neck."

The woman laughed, saying, "You crack me up, Martin. I swear you do."

It's a common mistake for vacationing Americans to assume that everyone around them is French and therefore speaks no English whatsoever. These two didn't seem like exceptionally mean people. Back home they probably would have had the decency to whisper, but here they felt free to say whatever they wanted, face-to-face and in a normal tone of voice. It was the same way someone might talk in front of a building or a painting they found particularly unpleasant. An experienced traveler could have told by looking at my shoes that I wasn't French. And even if I were French, it's not as if English is some mysterious tribal dialect spoken only by anthropologists and a small population of cannibals. They happen to teach English in schools all over the world. There are no eligibility requirements. Anyone can learn it. Even people who reportedly smell bad despite the fact that they've just taken a bath and are wearing clean clothes.

Because they had used the tiresome word *froggy* and complained about my odor, I was now licensed to hate this couple as much as I wanted. This made me happy, as I'd wanted to hate them from the moment I'd entered the subway car and seen them hugging the pole. Unleashed by their insults, I was now free to criticize Martin's clothing: the pleated denim shorts, the baseball cap, the T-shirt advertising a San Diego pizza restaurant. Sunglasses hung from his neck on a fluorescent cable, and the couple's bright new his-and-her sneakers suggested that they might be headed somewhere dressy for dinner. Comfort has its place, but it seems rude to visit another country dressed as if you've come to mow its lawns.

The man named Martin was in the process of showing the woman what he referred to as "my Paris." He looked at the subway map and announced that at some point during their stay, he'd maybe take her to the Louvre, which he pronounced as having two distinct syllables. *Loov-rah.* I'm hardly qualified to belittle anyone else's pronunciation, but he was setting himself up by acting like such an expert. "Yeah," he said, letting out a breath, "I thought we might head over there some day this week and do some nosing around. It's not for everyone, but something tells me you might like it."

People are often frightened of Parisians, but an American in Paris will find no harsher critic than another American. France isn't even my country, but there I was, deciding that these people needed to be sent back home, preferably in chains. In disliking them, I was forced to recognize my own pretension, and that made me hate them even more. The train took a curve, and when I moved my hand farther up the pole, the man turned to the woman, saying, "Carol — hey, Carol, watch out. That guy's going after your wallet."

"What?"

"Your wallet," Martin said. "That joker's trying to steal your wallet. Move your pocketbook to the front where he can't get at it."

She froze, and he repeated himself, barking, "The front. Move your pocketbook around to the front. Do it now. The guy's a pickpocket."

The woman named Carol grabbed for the strap on her shoulder and moved her pocketbook so that it now rested on her stomach. "Wow," she said. "I sure didn't see *that* coming."

"Well, you've never been to Paris before, but let that be a lesson to you." Martin glared at me, his eyes narrowed to slits. "This city is full of stinkpots like our little friend here. Let your guard down, and they'll take you for everything you've got."

Now I was a stinkpot *and* a thief. It occurred to me to say something, but I thought it might be better to wait and see what he came up with next. Another few minutes, and he might have decided I was a crack dealer or a white slaver. Besides, if I said something at this point, he probably would have apologized, and I wasn't interested in that. His embarrassment would have pleased me, but once he recovered, there would be that awkward period that sometimes culminates in a handshake. I didn't want to touch these people's hands or see things from their point of view, I just wanted to continue hating them. So I kept my mouth shut and stared off into space.

The train stopped at the next station. Passengers got off, and Carol and Martin moved to occupy two folding seats located beside the door. I thought they might ease on to another topic, but Martin was on a roll now, and there was no stopping him. "It was some shithead like him that stole my wallet on my last trip to Paris," he said, nodding his head in my direction. "He got me on the subway — came up from behind, and I never felt a thing. Cash, credit cards, driver's license: *poof* — all of it gone, just like that."

I pictured a scoreboard reading MARTY 0 STINKPOTS 1, and clenched my fist in support of the home team.

"What you've got to understand is that these creeps are practiced professionals," he said. "I mean, they've really got it down to an art, if you can call that an art form."

"I wouldn't call it an art form," Carol said. "Art is beautiful, but taking people's wallets . . . that stinks, in my opinion."

"You've got that right," Martin said. "The thing is that these jokers usually work in pairs." He squinted toward the opposite end of the train. "Odds are that he's probably got a partner somewhere on this subway car."

"You think so?"

"I know so," he said. "They usually time it so that one of them clips your wallet just as the train pulls into the station.

The other guy's job is to run interference and trip you up once you catch wind of what's going on. Then the train stops, the doors open, and they disappear into the crowd. If Stinky there had gotten his way, he'd probably be halfway to Timbuktu by now. I mean, make no mistake, these guys are fast."

I'm not the sort of person normally mistaken for being fast and well-coordinated, and because of this, I found Martin's assumption to be oddly flattering. Stealing wallets was nothing to be proud of, but I like being thought of as cunning and professional. I'd been up until 4 A.M. the night before, reading a book about recluse spiders, but to him the circles beneath my eyes likely reflected a long evening spent snatching flies out of the air, or whatever it is that pickpockets do for practice.

"The meatball," he said. "Look at him, just standing there waiting for his next victim. If I had my way, he'd be picking pockets with his teeth. An eye for an eye, that's what I say. Someone ought to chop the guy's hands off and feed them to the dogs."

Oh, I thought, *but first you'll have to catch me.*

"It just gets my goat," he said, "I mean, where's a *policioni* when you need one?"

Policioni? Where did he think he was? I tried to imagine Martin's conversation with a French policeman and pictured him waving his arms, shouting, "That man tried to picka my frienda's pocketoni!" I wanted very much to hear such a conversation and decided I would take the wallet from Hugh's back pocket as we left the train. Martin would watch me steal from a supposed stranger and most likely would intercede. He'd put me in a headlock or yell for help, and when a crowd gathered, I'd say, "What's the problem? Is it against the law to borrow money from my boyfriend?" If the police came, Hugh would explain the situation in his perfect French while I'd toss in a few of my most polished phrases. "That guy's crazy," I'd say, pointing at Martin. "I think he's drunk. Look at how his face is swollen." I was practicing these lines to myself when Hugh came up from behind and tapped me on the shoulder, signaling that the next stop was ours.

"There you go," Martin said. "That's him, that's the part-ner. Didn't I tell you he was around here somewhere? They always work in pairs. It's the oldest trick in the book."

Hugh had been reading the paper and had no idea what had been going on. It was too late now to pretend to pick his pocket, and I was stuck without a decent backup plan. As we pulled into the station, I recalled an afternoon ten years ear-lier. I'd been riding the Chicago el with my sister Amy, who was getting off three or four stops ahead of me. The doors opened, and as she stepped out of the crowded car, she turned around to yell, "So long, David. Good luck beating that rape charge." Everyone onboard had turned to stare at me. Some seemed curious, some seemed frightened, but the over-whelming majority appeared to hate me with a passion I had never before encountered. "That's my sister," I'd said. "She likes to joke around." I laughed and smiled, but it did no good. Every gesture made me appear more guilty, and I wound up getting off at the next stop rather than continue riding alongside people who thought of me as a rapist. I wanted to say something that good to Martin, but I can't think as fast as Amy. In the end this man would go home warning his friends to watch out for pickpockets in Paris. He'd be the same old Martin, but at least for the next few seconds, I still had the opportunity to be somebody different, somebody quick and dangerous.

The dangerous me noticed how Martin tightened his fists when the train pulled to a stop. Carol held her pocketbook close against her chest and sucked in her breath as Hugh and I stepped out of the car, no longer finicky little boyfriends on their overseas experiment, but rogues, accomplices, halfway to Timbuktu.

I Almost Saw This Girl
Get Killed

I ONCE OWNED A BOOK designed to provoke the imagination and help bored children discover constructive ways to pass the time. Though ultimately no great shakes, the projects were proposed and illustrated with such enthusiasm that even the most hardened ten-year-old could be tricked into believing he was in for some serious fun. "Why not construct ghosts out of leftover gift wrap?" the book would suggest. "Why not decorate your desktop with a school bus made from a brick!"

I thought of this book when Hugh and I attended the Festival of Saint Anne, a local fair held in a neighboring village, not far from our house in Normandy. Here was an event that answered the question "Why?" with a resounding "Why not!"

"Why not grab a hot glue gun and attach seashells to flowerpots?" asked the industrious grandmothers manning the crafts table. "Why not crochet long woollen sausages and lay them at the foot of the door to ward off drafts?"

There were a few low-key rides, and a game in which players threw tennis balls at papier-mâché likenesses of Idi Amin and Richard Nixon. Then there was the feature attraction, which posed the question "Why not build an arena and spend some time with angry cows?"

The cows in question were lean, long-horned teenagers known as *vachettes*. Bullish in both appearance and temperament, they're the juvenile delinquents of the cow family, the dirt-farming cousins who sleep in trailers and fight like men. Offer a vachette a shot of liquor, and she'll probably take it. Mention a vachette to one of the local Normand dairy cows, and she'll roll her long-lashed eyes, saying, "Well, *really*."

The woman at the gate explained that should Hugh and I volunteer to participate, that is, to spend time with one of these angry young cows, our admission fees would be waived. All we needed to do was sign a few simple documents, effectively clearing the festival organizers of any liability. Being a volunteer meant that in exchange for a possible spinal cord injury, we could each save the equivalent of four American dollars. "Come on," the woman said, "it'll be fun."

I pictured a handsome French doctor explaining the standard colostomy procedure, and then I disappointed the woman at the gate by pulling out my wallet. We paid our admission and joined the hundred-odd spectators seated on the collapsible bleachers. They were our neighbors, the people we saw while standing in line at the bakery and the hardware store. The mayor breezed by, followed by the postman and the train conductor, and each of them stopped to say hello. While others might find it stifling, I like the storybook quality intrinsic to village life. The butcher, the stonemason, the sheep farmer, and the schoolmarm: it's as though these figures came in a box along with pint-size storefronts and little stone houses. In a world where everyone is known by their occupations, Hugh and I are consistently referred to as "the Americans," as if possessing a blue passport was so much work that it left us with no time for anything else. As with the English and the Parisians, we're the figurines who move into the little stone houses once the tailor flies out the car window or the cabinetmaker has his head chewed off by the teething dog. Sold separately, we are greeted with an equal mix of curiosity, civility, and resignation.

Tiered benches had been erected in what was normally a pasture, and they afforded a view of a spacious plywood arena in which a dozen young men engaged in a game of soccer. I thought maybe we'd arrived too late and had missed the main attraction, but then someone opened the door of the cattle trailer and a vachette raced down the ramp and pounded on to the field. She paused briefly to get her bearings and then she attacked, astounding the audience with her speed and single-minded sense of purpose. Unburdened by a dairy cow's timidity and great bother of fat, she charged the soccer players as if seeking revenge in the name of oppressed cattle the world over. The young men scattered and ran for cover, occasionally darting from their protective barricades to give the ball another fleeting whack. This was pretty much the way things went for the rest of the afternoon. The vachettes charged, the volunteers ran for their lives, and the audience cheered. It differed from a bullfight in that there was no element of skill or pretense of two equally matched opponents. The playing field was clearly uneven, both figuratively and literally. A vachette might chip a horn or pull a neck muscle while throwing a volunteer over her head. She might scuff a hoof kicking someone in the skull, but otherwise she risked no real danger. The ambulance parked beside the concession stand was clearly not waiting for her, and she seemed to know it. On the other hand, it was hard to work up much sympathy for the volunteers who had knowingly agreed to torment a dangerous animal.

The afternoon had just begun, but already I was wondering how I might feel if someone were to get seriously hurt — maybe not killed or paralyzed — but definitely injured. Just as important, how would I feel if someone *didn't* get hurt? Wasn't that the promise of spending time with a vachette? If it was cuteness we were after, they'd be playing soccer against a newborn kitten. My hopes had nothing to do with these men in particular. I had nothing against any of them and did not actively wish them harm. I was just struggling with my inner vachette and pondering the depths of my own inhumanity.

My conscience had been bothering me for about a

month, ever since the evening Hugh and I had attended a large, headachy fair held each year in Paris. We'd been walking down the midway when I noticed one of the rides frozen in mid motion, several of the passengers just sort of dangling there. This didn't strike me as unusual, as the creators of these rides seemed to have taken the extra step in making their attractions just that much more hideous than they needed to be. If something whipped back and forth, it also needed to spin on an axis, bob up and down, and hurl through a jet spray of filthy water. Every effort had been made to leave the passengers as nauseous as possible, and the crowds seemed to love it. On first seeing the broken ride, I'd assumed it was designed to pause at frequent intervals, allowing those onboard to feel the full effect of their discomfort. I turned to watch a blue-faced teenager projectile vomit against the side of a taffy stand, and when I looked back up, I noticed that the ride was still not moving and that a crowd had begun to gather.

I don't know what happens to people when this ride is working, but when it isn't, the passengers hang in the air at odd angles, harnessed into legless metal love seats. A couple lay twelve feet off the ground, their seat back stuck in a horizontal position, staring up at the sky as if undergoing some kind of examination. Higher up, maybe fifty feet in the air, a young woman with long blond hair was hanging facedown, held in place by nothing but the harness that now strained against her weight. The couple at least had each other; it was the young woman who seemed the most likely candidate for tragedy. The crowd moved closer, and if the other three to four hundred people were anything like me, they watched the young woman and thought of the gruesome story they'd eventually relate to friends over drinks or dinner. In the not-too-distant future, whenever the conversation turned to the subject of fairs or amusement parks, I'd wait until my companions had finished their mediocre anecdotes and then, at just the right moment, almost as an afterthought, I'd say, "I once saw a girl fall to her death from one of those rides."

I estimated the hush that might follow my opening sentence and felt my future listeners leaning forward, just slightly, in their seats. The dead woman was nobody I knew personally, and this would free my audience from having to feel awkward or embarrassed for having broached the subject in the first place. They'd ask questions, and my detailed answers would leave them feeling shaken and oddly satisfied. I voiced these thoughts to Hugh, who denounced both me and the crowd, unironically characterizing the atmosphere as "carnival-like." He left the midway, and I moved closer to the foot of the ride, pressing against others who, like me, watched the night sky while wearing an expression most people reserve for fireworks. The blond woman's shoe came off, and we watched it fall to the ground. "And then one of her shoes came off," I heard myself saying. I don't know that I've ever felt so cheap, but I rationalized it by reminding myself that it wasn't my fault this person was trapped. I hadn't told her to go on the ride. The management clearly had no plan for getting her down, but that wasn't my fault, either. I told myself that my interest was compassionate and that my presence amounted to a demonstration of support. I didn't know about the others, but I was needed.

The police arrived, and I took offense when they shouted that this was not a show. *Well of course it's not,* I thought. *But that shouldn't diminish my investment.* I'd been there much longer than they had. I'd been waiting patiently for something to happen, and it wasn't fair for them to herd me away just to make room for some alleged firetruck or ambulance. The crowd stood its ground, and then more policemen arrived, shoving and herding us back out on to the midway, where our view was soon blocked by emergency vehicles. I was ready to start crying, but everyone else seemed to take their disappointment in stride. The mob dispersed, and people headed off to other, equally dangerous rides where they were strapped into harnesses and jerked into the sky to tempt their own untimely deaths. On the way home that night I practiced saying, "I almost saw this girl get killed." I tried it both in French and in English but found my enthusiasm waned after the word *almost.* Who cares about almost seeing someone die? I blamed the police for ruining my evening and tried to imagine what I might have felt if I *had* seen the young woman fall.

Morally speaking, the vachette arena felt a lot less muddy than the carnival midway. I wasn't sitting in the stands because someone had been hurt. I was simply watching a scheduled event alongside other members of the community. If someone were to get killed, I wouldn't be rubbernecking but just plain old flesh necking.

I never quite understood the soccer match. The volunteers weren't playing against the cow, they were just attempting to play in her presence. Nobody scored any goals, and I felt nothing but confusion when time was called and another, equally puzzling activity was introduced. In round two the contestants were given dozens of inner tubes and instructed to stack them into tall, puffy towers, which were immediately knocked down by the afternoon's second vachette. Something about the inner tubes seemed to disturb her deeply, and she attacked them with frightening gusto. The young men raced about the field attempting to construct their separate towers. They tried to keep ahead of the animal, but when the clock ran out, they had nothing to show for their efforts.

A break was called, and I was introduced to the man seated beside me, a retired roofer who explained that the vachettes were from a small town in southern France, not far from the Spanish border. Bred for hostility, they traveled from town to town performing what was called "the traditional vachette program." It was the word *traditional* that got to me, the thought that inner-tube towers had been constructed for years and that it just wouldn't be the same without them. I don't know who came up with the traditional vachette program, but I'm willing to bet that he had some outstanding drug connections. How else could a person come up with this stuff? One game involved trying to pull a decorative bow from a vachette's head, and another seemed to amount to nothing more than name-calling. The only ones who appeared to understand the rules were the vachettes themselves, whose instructions seemed pretty straightforward: attack, attack, attack. It wasn't until the sixth event of the afternoon that two of the contestants were finally injured. For reasons that made no sense whatsoever, a sizable pool had been constructed in the center of the arena, made by laying a great sheet of plastic over a square foundation of hay bales. An enormous truck had been brought in, the pool had been filled, and the volunteers had been trying to coax their latest vachette into the water. She'd kept the majority of her opponents cowering behind their barricades until the last few minutes of the event, when a young man in a floppy hat decided to make a run for it. The vachette looked the other way, pretending to admire a herd of friendly cows grazing in the distance, and then, her head lowered, she charged, catching the contestant in the lower back and jabbing him, tossing him with her long, crooked horns. As the young man fell to the ground, I involuntarily grabbed the knees of both Hugh and the retired roofer. I grabbed them and then gave out a little high-pitched cry, similar to that of a rabbit. A second volunteer ran on to the field, hoping to create a distraction, and the vachette ran him over, returning moments later to deliver a few swift kicks that effectively broke two of the young man's ribs. She looked ready to disembowel him and might have done so had her handlers not lured her back into her trailer.

The fact that the roofer had to pry my hand off his knee is proof that my inner vachette was not nearly as vicious as I'd imagined her to be. The show over, I sat trembling in the stands, watching the contestants who now gathered around the concession booth showing their battle scars to anyone who would look. The horn-in-the-back injury wasn't nearly as bad as I'd imagined. The victim had to lower his trousers in order to exhibit the wound, which amounted to little more than an angry red welt located just to the right of his crack. Wincing slightly, the fellow with the broken ribs decided he would wait until morning to visit the hospital. He and the others were enjoying their moment in the sun and saw no reason to cut it short. Surrounded by their admiring neighbors, they reenacted the more dramatic moments of the afternoon and speculated on how they might do things differently the next time. They drank and joked and were still at it when Hugh and I returned later that evening for the fireworks display. It wasn't much in terms of a spectacle. I've seen more elaborate pyrotechnics at the grand openings of grocery stores, but the audience was kind and everyone made an effort to pretend that the display was magnificent. Between the puny pops of Roman candles and the hisses of launching rockets, we could hear the vachettes bitterly lowing from within their nearby trailer. They would leave the following morning to wreak their havoc at some other backwater festival, where another set of figures would end their evening gathered before their perfect matchbox village, pointing to the sky and whispering, "Ohhh. Ahhh."

The incident at the fair had caused me to worry that perhaps my vachometer was reading a little higher than anyone else's, and it pleased me to realize that, at the time they were hit, I'd been rooting for the young men down on the field. Their injuries turned out to be relatively minor, but still I'd felt no pleasure witnessing their misfortune. I wondered how I might have reacted had somebody been killed, but then I dismissed the thought as overly dramatic. Watching even the sorriest of sporting events bears no resemblance to coming upon an accident and hoping to exploit it for your own personal gain. Anyway, it had been the young blond woman who'd wound up with the most disturbing story. We might have watched her, hanging by a strap umpteen feet in the air, but, even worse, she had been forced to watch us. Squinting down at our hideous, expectant faces, she probably saw no real reason to return to earth and reclaim her life among scumbags like us. For all I know, she might still be there, hovering above Paris and kicking, scratching at anyone who tries to get near her.

Smart Guy

WHEN I WAS TWENTY-FIVE, I found a job cleaning construction sites in the suburbs of Raleigh. It was dull work, made even duller on the days I was partnered with a fellow named Reggie, an alleged genius unhappy with the course his life had taken. Every day he'd talk about how smart he was, and it was always the same conversation.

"Here I am with a one-thirty IQ, and they've got me sweeping up sawdust." He'd glare at the bristles of his broom as if they had conspired to hold him back. "Can you beat that? A one-thirty! I'm serious, man. I've been tested."

This was my cue to act impressed, but I generally passed.

"One three oh," he'd say. "In case you didn't know it, that's genius level. With a mind like mine, I could be *doing* something, you know what I mean?"

"Absolutely."

"Pulling nails out of two by fours is not what I was made for."

"I hear you."

"A sixty could do what I'm doing. That leaves me with seventy extra IQ points sitting around in my head doing nothing."

"They must be bored."

"You're damn right they are," he'd say. "People like me need to be challenged."

"Maybe you could turn on the fan and sweep against the wind," I'd suggest. "That's pretty difficult."

"Don't make fun of me. I'm a lot smarter than you."

"How do you know?" I'd ask. "I might be a three hundred or something."

"A three hundred. Right. There's no such thing as a three hundred. I'd place you at around seventy-two, tops."

"What does that mean?" I'd ask.

"It means I hope you like pushing a broom."

"And what does *that* mean?"

He'd shake his head in pity. "Ask me in about fifteen years."

Fifteen years later I found myself working for a house-cleaning company. Yes, it was unskilled labor, but for what it's worth, I did very little sweeping. Mainly I vacuumed. Oh, but that was years ago. Two years ago, to be exact.

I'm not sure what Reggie is doing now, but I thought of him when, at the age of forty-two, I finally had my IQ tested.

Being an adult with a fairly steady history of supporting myself, I figured the test could do no real harm. At this stage in my life, the die has already been cast and, no matter how dumb I am, I'm obviously smart enough to get by. I failed to realize that intelligence tests effectively muck with both your past and your future, clarifying a lifetime of bad choices and setting you up for the inevitability of future failure. When I think of an IQ test, I now picture a pickle-nosed sorceress, turning from her kettle to ask, "Are you *sure* you want the answer to that question?"

I said yes, and as a result, I can still hear the witch's shrill cackle every time I reach for a broom.

As a child I'd always harbored a sneaking suspicion that I might be a genius. The theory was completely my own, corroborated by no one, but so what? Being misunderstood was all part of the package. My father occasionally referred to me as "Smart Guy," but eventually I realized that when saying it, he usually meant just the opposite.

"Hey, Smart Guy — coating your face with mayonnaise because you can't find the insect repellent."

"Hey, Smart Guy, thinking you can toast marshmallows in your bedroom."

That type of thing.

I thought I could cure diabetes by spreading suntan lotion on sticks of chewing gum. Sea & Ski on Juicy Fruit, Coppertone on Big Red. I had the raw ingredients *and* a test subject, all under the same roof.

"Hey, Smart Guy," my father would say, "offer your

grandmother another piece of that gum, and *you'll* be the one scrubbing your teeth in the bathroom sink."

What did *he* know?

Alone in my bedroom, I studied pictures of intelligent men and searched for a common denominator. There was a definite Smart Guy look, but it was difficult to get just right. Throw away your comb, and you could resemble either Albert Einstein or Larry Fine. Both wore rumpled suits and stuck out their tongues, but only one displayed true genius in such films as *Booty and the Beast* and *The Three Stooges Meet Hercules.*

My grades sank, teachers laughed in my face, but I tried not to let it get to me. In high school I flirted with the idea that I might be a philosophical genius. According to me and several of my friends, it was almost scary the way I could read people. I practiced thoughtfully removing my glasses and imagined myself appearing on one of those Sunday-morning television shows, where I'd take my seat beside other learned men and voice my dark and radical theories on the human condition.

"People are insecure," I'd say. "They wear masks and play games."

My ideas would be like demons rushing from a hellish cave, and my fellow intellectuals, startled by the truth and enormity of my observations, would try to bottle them up before they spread.

"'That's enough!" they'd yell. "For the love of God, somebody silence him!"

Far scarier than any of my ideas is the fact that, at the age of seventeen, I was probably operating at my intellectual peak. I should have been tested then, before I squandered what little sense I had. By the time I reached my thirties, my brain had been strip-mined by a combination of drugs, alcohol, and the chemical solvents used at the refinishing company where I worked. Still, there were moments when, against all reason, I thought I might be a genius. These moments were provoked not by any particular accomplishment but by cocaine and crystal methamphetamine — drugs that allow you to lean over a mirror with a straw up your nose, suck up an entire week's paycheck, and think, "God, I'm smart."

It's always been the little things that encourage me. I'll watch a movie in which an attractive woman in a sports bra, a handsome widower, and a pair of weak-chinned cowards are pursued by mighty reptiles or visitors from another galaxy. "The cowards are going to die," I'll think, and then when they do, I congratulate myself on my intelligence. When I say, "Oh, that was so predictable," it sounds brainy and farsighted. When other people say it, it sounds stupid. Call me an egghead, but that's how I see it.

It was curiosity that led me to take my IQ test. Simple, stupid, brutal curiosity, the same thing that motivates boys to see what flies might look like without their wings. I took my test in Paris, in the basement of an engineering school not far from my apartment. I'd figured that, on its own, my score would mean nothing — I needed someone to compare myself with — and so Hugh came along and took the test as well. I'd worried that he might score higher than me, but a series of recent events had set me at ease. A week earlier, while vacationing in Slovenia, he'd ordered a pizza that the English-speaking waiter had strenuously recommend he avoid. It came topped with a mound of canned vegetables: peas, corn, carrot coins, potatoes, and diced turnips. Observing the look of dumb horror on his face as the waiter delivered the ugly pizza, I decided that, in a test of basic intelligence, I was a definite shoo-in. A few days later, with no trace of irony, he suggested that the history of the chocolate chip might make for an exciting musical. "If, of course, you found the right choreographer."

"Yes," I'd said. "Of course."

The tests we took were designed to determine our eligibility for Mensa, an international association for those with IQs of 132 or higher. Its members come from all walks of life and get together every few weeks to take in a movie or enjoy a weenie roast. They're like Elks or Masons, only they're smart. Our tests were administered by an attractive French psychologist named Madame Haberman, who was herself a Mensa member. She explained that we'd be taking four tests, each of them timed. In order to qualify for Mensa membership, we'd need to score in the top 2 percent of any given one. "All right then," she said. "Are we ready?"

I've known people who have taken IQ tests in the past, and whenever I've asked them to repeat one of the questions, they've always drawn a blank, saying, "Oh, you know, they were . . . multiple-choice things." Immediately after taking my test, I was hard-pressed to recall much of anything except the remarkable sense of relief I'd felt each time the alarm went off and we were asked to put down our pencils. The tests were printed in little booklets. In the first, we were shown a series of three drawings and asked which of the four adjacent ones might best complete the sequence. The sample question pictured a leaf standing top to bottom and progressively leaning to the right. It's the only question I remember, and probably the only question I answered correctly. The second test had to do with spatial relationships and left me with a headache that would last for the next twenty-four hours. In the third test we were told to examine five drawings and figure out which two didn't belong. Eventually a break was called, and we stepped out into the street. Hugh and Madame Haberman discussed her upcoming trip to the Turkish coast, but I was still trapped in test world. Five deaf students walked down the street, and I tried to determine which two did not belong. I imagined myself approaching the two boys wearing tennis shoes and pictured their confusion as I laid my hands upon their shoulders, saying, "I'm going to have to ask you to come with me."

Our final test involved determining a pattern in four pairs of dominoes and prophesying what the fifth pair might look like. There were pages of questions, and I didn't even come close to finishing. I'd like to say that the room was too hot or that Madame Haberman distracted me with her incessant banjo picking, but none of this is true. According to the rules of Mensa France, the test instructions were delivered in French, but I understood every word. I have no one but myself to blame.

A week after taking the tests, our scores arrived in the mail. Hugh has been advised to try again: scores can fluctuate according to stress and circumstance, and he's right on the cusp of Mensa qualification. My letter began with the words, "Dear Monsieur Sedaris, We regret to inform you . . ."

It turns out that I'm really stupid, practically an idiot. There are cats that weigh more than my IQ score. Were my number translated into dollars, it would buy you about three buckets of fried chicken. The fact that this surprises me only bespeaks the depths of my ignorance.

The tests reflected my ability to reason logically. Either you reason things out or you don't. Those who do, have high IQs. Those who don't reach for the mayonnaise when they can't find the insect repellent. When I became upset over my test score, Hugh explained that everybody thinks differently — I just happen to do it a lot less than the average adult.

"Think donkey," he said. "Then take it down a few notches."

It's a point I can't really argue. My brain wants nothing to do with reason. It never has. If I was told to vacate my apartment by next week, I wouldn't ask around or consult the real estate listings. Instead, I'd just imagine myself living in a moated sugar-cube castle, floating from room to room on a king-size magic carpet. If I have one saving grace, it's that I'm lucky enough to have found someone willing to handle the ugly business of day-to-day living.

Hugh consoled me, saying, "Don't let it get to you. There are plenty of things you're good at."

When asked for some examples, he listed vacuuming and naming stuffed animals. He says he can probably come up with a few more, but he'll need some time to think.

The Late Show

I'M THINKING OF MAKING a little jacket for my clock radio. Nothing fancy or permanent, just something casual it can slip into during the wee hours. I'm not out to match it with the curtains or disguise it to look like something it's not. The problem is not that the clock radio feels underdressed, the problem is that I cannot bear to watch the numbers advance in the heartless way common to this particular model. Time doesn't fly — it flaps, the numbers turning on a wheel that operates much like the gears on a stretching rack.

For the first twenty years of my life I rocked myself to sleep. It was a harmless enough hobby, but eventually I had to give it up. Throughout the next twenty-two years I lay still and discovered that after a few minutes I could drop off with no problem. Follow seven beers with a couple of scotches and a thimble of good marijuana, and it's funny how sleep just sort of comes on its own. Often I never even made it to bed. I'd squat down to pet the cat and wake up on the floor eight hours later, having lost a perfectly good excuse to change my clothes. I'm now told that this is not called "going to sleep" but rather "passing out," a phrase that carries a distinct hint of judgment.

As a perverse and incredibly boring experiment, I am now trying to prove that I can get by without the drugs and the drinking. It was hard for the first few months, but then I discovered that I *can* live without these things. It's a pretty miserable excuse for a life, but technically it still qualifies. My heart continues to pump. I can put socks on my feet and make ice; I just can't sleep.

I've never gone to bed early, and have no intention of changing my schedule. There's always a little hump at about eleven o'clock, which I've traditionally gotten over by drinking a lot of something. I'm used to holding a glass or can and raising it to my mouth every thirty seconds or so. It's a habit my right hand can't seem to break.

Having decided in advance that I will never use the word *decaf,* I began looking for a new beverage. My disappointing search taught me that, without the blessing of vodka, tomato juice is a complete waste of time. Even when you buy it in a bottle, it still tastes like the can. I've learned that soda gives me a stomachache, grape juice gives me a headache, and that nothing is more disgusting than a glass of milk, especially French milk, which comes in a box and can sit unrefrigerated for five months, at which point it simply turns into cheese and is moved to a different section of the grocery store.

Following a brief and unsatisfying flirtation with lemon-tainted water, I finally settled on tea, which is something I'd never placed beside coffee in terms of things that will keep you awake. I've never been one of those people who talk about a "sugar rush" or claim to feel the immediate effect of a vitamin tablet. I'm not terribly in touch with my body but have noticed that, taken in great quantities, tea is actually pretty serious. Drink twelve cups at about eleven P.M., and you'll really notice the difference between going to bed and going to sleep. Even if you're lucky enough to lose consciousness, you'll find you still need to get up every half hour just to empty your bladder.

So here lies the new me. It's 5:48 in the morning, I'm thinking of making an outfit for my clock radio, and I'm so full of caffeine that my scalp itches. To read a book or attempt a crossword puzzle would be an admission of defeat, and I know that if I let my mind wander, it would most likely head off in the direction of the liquor cabinet. Rather than practicing my irregular verbs or trying to make sense of my day, I pass the time by replaying one of my current, ongoing fantasies. These are the epic daydreams I would normally call forth while walking around town or waiting in line at the grocery store. They're like movies I edit and embroider and watch over and over again, regularly recasting the villains and updating the minor details. My current inventory is more than enough to keep me busy, and includes the following titles:

Mr. Science

Alone in my basement laboratory, I invent a serum that causes trees to grow at ten times their normal rate, meaning that a person can plant a sapling and enjoy its fruit or shade one year later. It really is a perfect idea. Nobody likes waiting for a tree to grow — that's why more people don't plant them; it seems hopeless. By the time they've matured, you've either died or moved to a retirement home.

My trees grow at an advanced rate for anywhere from two to five years before tapering off to normal, and they are a wild success. Instant parks are created. Cities and subdevelopments are transformed seemingly overnight, and the hurricane states erect statues in my honor. Frustrated parents attempt to use my serum on their children, but it doesn't work on people. "Sorry," I say, "but there's no cure for adolescence." The lumberjacks and environmentalists love me equally, but a problem arises when a group of lesser scientists spread the rumor that the leaves of my trees cause cancer in laboratory animals. I then discover a cure for cancer just so I can say, "What was that you were carrying on about?"

The Mr. Science look changes from one night to the next. Sometimes I'm tall and fair-skinned. Sometimes I'm dark and stocky. The only constant is my hair, which is always thick and straight, cut in such a way that if surfacing from a dive, my bangs would fall to my lower lip. I keep it combed back, but every so often a lock will break free and hang like a whiplash down the side of my face. Mine is a look of intense concentration, the face of a man who's forever trying to re- call an old locker combination. When receiving my Nobel Prize, I'm so lost in thought that the peacenik seated beside me has to elbow me in the ribs, saying, "Hey, buddy, I think they're calling your name."

I'll sometimes have dinner with a group of happily cured cancer patients, but for the most part I tend to keep to myself, ignoring the great mound of social invitations heaped upon my desk. Without making any great fuss about it, I cure AIDS and emphysema, meaning that people can once again enjoy a cigarette after a rigorous bout of anal sex. There will be a lot of talk about "turning back the clock," most of it done by people whose clocks will not be affected one way or another. Psychologists will appear on TV, suggesting that our former AIDS and cancer patients are desperately in need of counseling. "We have to teach these people that it's okay to live again," they'll say. Their self-serving message will be met with great peals of laughter, as will the flood of books with titles such as *Getting Over Getting Better* and *Remission Impos- sible: The Conflict of Identity in a Post-Cancer Society*. After decades of falling for such nonsense, the American people will decide they've had enough pointless anxiety. Antidepressants will go out of style, and filthy jokes will enjoy a much-de- served comeback.

I cure paralysis because I'm tired of watching skateboarders race down the wheelchair ramps, and I cure muscular dystrophy just to get rid of the Jerry Lewis telethon. I eradicate mental retardation so no one will ever again have an excuse to make a movie based upon an old television series, and I cure diabetes, herpes, and Parkinson's disease as personal favors to some of my favorite celebrities. I invent a pill that will allow you to drink seawater, and another that will erase the effects of either twelve cups of tea or seven beers and two scotches.

All my discoveries make headlines, but the most controversial is a soap that rejuvenates aging skin. You take a bath or shower, lather yourself with my product, let it sit for three minutes, and once it's rinsed off, you look as though you're twenty-five years old. The effects last for three days, and the process can be repeated indefinitely. The soap is insanely expensive, and everybody over the age of forty simply has to have it. Suddenly, nursing-home residents resemble oddly dressed graduate students, and beautiful women in adult diapers are driving very slowly and blocking the grocery store aisles with their carts. I like imagining the confusion my product will generate: the startled look of the authentic young single as his date deposits her teeth in a bedside jar, the baby-faced eighty-year-old forgetting he'd agreed to play Father Time at the New Year's party. Former beauty queens will attempt to reclaim their titles, and no one will suspect a thing until the talent competition, when they offer their renditions of "Sonny Boy" and "Ain't We Got Fun."

Sadly, my soap will not work on everyone. If you've had

a lot of cosmetic surgery in the past — your eyes lifted, your wrinkles pumped with collagen — your youthful self will appear freakish and catlike, like one of those aliens rumored to have visited the town of Roswell, New Mexico. For reasons that confound medical science, the product also fails to affect those working in certain professions — the editors of fashion magazines, for example. Here are people who have spent their lives promoting youthful beauty, making everyone over the age of thirty feel like an open sore. Now, too late, they'll attempt to promote liver spots as the season's most sophisticated accessory. "Old is the new young," they'll say, but nobody will listen to them. Television executives will also be left out, especially those whose job it is to move a program from Sunday at eight to Wednesday at nine-thirty, then back to Sunday and on to Thursday, all so they can sell a few more soft-drink or taco commercials. When petitioned by these people to please, for the love of God, come up with something that can help them, I'll redesign that goofy plastic bird that perpetually lowers its head into a little cup of water. My version will work just like the old one but — get this — it'll be wearing a pair of sunglasses!

With the money I make from my numerous inventions, I build my own spaceship and discover another planet that looks a lot like Earth and is only twenty minutes away. My new world has real estate developers and multinational corporations foaming at the mouth, and I like to imagine the meetings during which they try to explain why the universe needs another Pizza Hut or Six Flags amusement park. I'll listen to their presentations and lead them on a bit before suggesting that the recently named Planet Fuck You Up the Ass with a Sharp Stick might not be for everyone.

The Knockout

I'm one fight away from being named heavyweight boxing champion of the world, and still people are asking, "Who *is* this guy?" If forced to describe me to a police sketch artist, you might begin by mentioning my nose. It isn't exactly up-turned, it isn't "pugged"; but when they're viewed eye to eye, you'll notice that my nostrils are prominent and oddly expressive, like a second, smaller pair of eyes assigned to keep watch over the lower half of my face, home to my full lips and perfect, luminous teeth.

When the sketch artist draws my eyes, you'll step back, saying, "No, I'm afraid that's not right at all." After four or five more unsuccessful attempts, the artist will lose his patience and remind you that "soulful" is not a precise physical description. The difficulty comes in trying to separate my eyes from my eyebrows, which alter my face much the way that varying punctuation marks can change the meaning of a sentence. I've got the exclamation point I wear when ambushed by photographers, the question mark, the period I wear when I mean business, the dash, the thoughtful semi-colon, and the series of three dots I rely upon when rudely interrupted or when searching for just the right word. The eyebrows work in consort with my inky black hair, which weighs in midway between curly and wavy, and calls for the invention of a new word.

"It's . . . cravy," you'll say. "Like a storm at sea if the ocean were made out of hair instead of water."

When the sketch artist throws down his pencil, you'll say, "Okay, then, how's this: he looks kind of like the guy who used to play Cord Roberts on the soap opera *One Life to Live*. Or, no, I take that back. He looks *exactly* like the guy who used to play Cord Roberts on *One Life to Live*. Is *that* descriptive enough for you?"

It's somewhat surprising that I'm a serious contender for the title of world heavyweight champion, not because I'm slow or weak but because I'm a relative newcomer to the sport. I'd been just another Yale medical student and had never really thought of fighting until I got shut out of an endotracheal intubation seminar and signed up for a boxing class instead. The teacher recognized my extraordinary talent, lined up a few regional matches, and one thing led to another. I looked good in a hooded sweatshirt, and so when asked to go professional, I said, "Okay. Why not?"

This fantasy takes care to avoid the more obvious *Rocky I–IV* comparisons. I never run around New Haven punching the air. Neither do I speak to turtles or greet friends with a nontraditional handshake. Most important, I'm never seen as an underdog. You have to care about something in order to hold that title, and I honestly don't give a damn one way or the other. For me, fighting is just a way to kill time until I get my medical degree and begin my residency. The boxing world feels cheated by my obvious lack of passion, but the press loves me. They're beside themselves because I'm white, and in writing about me they're able to express their racial anxieties while pretending not to. People who normally can't stand the idea of violence are suddenly willing to make an exception. Even the Mennonites place their bets and sign up for Pay-Per-View.

The championship bout is five days away when the public discovers I have a boyfriend, who maybe doesn't look like Hugh but definitely cooks like him. I haven't been hiding my homosexuality. I've never lied or purposely avoided the question, it's just that no one has ever specifically asked. I'd never seen it as any big deal, but the news seems to change everything. Those who loved me because I was white now feel betrayed. They'd assigned me to be their representative. I was supposed to kick some black ass in their name, but now they're not sure whose side they're on. Which is more important, my race or my sexual preference?

The question is answered when hate notes and truckloads of pansies are delivered to my training camp, the little sanctuary where I skip rope while listening to taped lectures on coronary collateralization and threadworm infection. The topics don't pertain to my specific area of study but, as I tell the reporters from *Ring* magazine, "I like to keep informed."

A clause in my contract states that before the big fight I must submit to a Barbara Walters interview, so I do. The first few minutes go pretty much as I'd expected. "What would you do if you were choking on a peanut?" she asks. "Show us how a real champ performs the Heimlich maneuver."

The hijinks over, we settle on to the sofa, where she clasps her hands and asks if it was hard for me to come out.

I know then that had Barbara Walters actually been choking on a peanut, I would have done nothing to help her. I hate the way the word *out* has been sexualized and forced into service for all things gay. When *out* is used as a verb, I start to hyperventilate. If some people are "outed," are other people "inned"? Can we say that someone has been "besided" or "overed"?

I have a similar adverse reaction when interviewed by the gay press. "No," I say, "I will not be entering the ring draped in a rainbow-striped flag." I must have been out of the country when they took the vote on that one. I abhor the rainbow stripe and would prefer something along the lines of a simple skull and crossbones. In the last few days before the fight, my eyebrows settle into a semipermanent question mark. I don't understand why I have to represent anyone. Whatever happened to winning the heavyweight championship for Hippocrates? Without really meaning to, I manage to alienate everyone but the endocrinologists, and even some of them are put off by a remark I made concerning blood calcium levels in hypoparathyroidism.

It goes without saying that I defeat the standing champion, but the mechanics of the fight never really interest me. I bleed a little, the other guy bleeds a lot, and then it's over.

If I really can't sleep, I kill time casting and recasting both my coach and the genetically altered Hugh. Then I play around with my retirement speech and decorate the waiting room of my doctor's office.

I've Got a Secret

I'm a pretty, slightly chubby White House intern who's had a brief affair with the president of the United States. Through no fault of my own, the details are leaked to the press, and within hours people are buying bumper stickers reading, SHAME ON YOU! and ANOTHER AMERICAN DISGUSTED BY PRESIDENT PLAYBOY.

My friends and family are shocked to learn that I had sex with a world leader. "Why didn't you tell us?" they ask, though they know it's a silly question. I've always been admired for my ability to keep a secret. I had a baby in high school, and no one ever found out about it. I gave birth in the woods behind my house and put the infant up for adoption just as soon as I'd cleaned myself off. Actually, I just left him in a box outside the agency door. It was a comfortable box, lined with blankets, and I hung around long enough to make sure he'd been found and taken inside. I'm not heartless, I just didn't want to leave a paper trail and have to worry that the child would grow up and come knocking at my door, expecting me to put him on my Christmas list.

Before it became front-page news, I'd almost forgotten that I'd had an affair with the president. It isn't that I sleep around a lot, it's just that, aside from the fact that he *is* the president, the relationship wasn't terribly memorable. I'm at home, defrosting my freezer and watching TV when my president interrupts a lousy speech on education to say, "I never had sex with that woman."

Yikes. *Okay,* I think, *so maybe I made a mistake. He's obviously not the man I thought he was.* I refill my ice cube trays and realize that life as I knew it is now officially over. Sixty years from now some doctor will tell his friends that he's just performed a hip replacement on the girl who slept with the president. That's what they'll call me from here on out, and the most I can do about it is try to set a good example. This will be accomplished by concentrating on my best assets and giving the country what it needs rather than what it wants.

With reporters camped outside my door, I can't really go anywhere, so I find a hardware store that delivers, and decide to paint my apartment. I'm going after the hard-to-reach places behind the radiator when the independent counsel arrives, promising that if I cooperate, I won't have to go to jail. "Well, that's a new one," I say. "Since when does anybody go to jail just for having sex with the president of the United States?" I tell the independent counsel exactly what I've told everybody else, which is nothing. Then I finish painting between the radiators, eat one last block of fudge, and lose twenty-five pounds.

When told I'd better hire a good attorney, I ask them to give me a public defender, whoever's available — it makes no difference to me. Why spend the rest of my life paying off my legal fees? I say nothing to the federal prosecutors and nothing to the reporters who call and send exotic flower arrangements, hoping I'll grant an interview or release a statement. They're claiming that I'll talk sooner or later, and it pleases me to know that they are wrong. I will never, for the rest of my life, say one word about my unfortunate affair with the president. I won't even mention the man's name. If it comes up in a crossword puzzle, I'll leave the spaces blank and work around them. He can run his mouth all he wants to, but someone needs to exercise a little control.

My public defender means well, but there's no way I'm going to testify in an outfit designed by Liz Claiborne. He's hoping to promote an image of quiet conservatism, but please! I'd rather go to the chair than appear before the entire world dressed like a department manager at Wall-Mart. Rather, I take my cue from *Gone with the Wind*: the scene in which Scarlett is forced to attend Miss Melanie's birthday party. She's just been caught behind the lumberyard with Ashley, and the whole town is talking about it. If she'd had her way, she would have stayed home, but Rhett Butler forces her to attend wearing a dress that screams *guilty* yet looks so good that you're left wondering why she'd ever lowered herself to chase after Ashley Wilkes.

Given the high visibility factor, every designer in the world wants to dress me for my grand-jury appearance. I go with one of the young English upstarts and choose a slightly exaggerated, magnificently tailored suit that emphasizes my new, waspy figure. Accessorized with the right mix of confidence and haughtiness, it reduces my audience to a world of leering carpetbaggers and gasping Aunt Pittypats. The moment I enter the courtroom it is understood that I am the most audacious and beautiful woman in the world. When called to the stand, I give nothing but my first and last names. The transcription will record that all subsequent questions were answered with either "You've got to be kidding" or "I honestly don't see how that's any of your business." The judge holds me in contempt, and the fashion press notes that my suit jacket neither strained nor bunched when my hands were cuffed behind my back.

I don't know how long they might sentence someone for refusing to disclose the details of an affair, but I imagine it wouldn't be more than a year or two. I do my time quietly but maintain a polite distance from those who would like to profit from my friendship. It looks really bad that the president allowed me to go to prison, and people will often try to tap what they imagine to be my considerable wellspring of anger. As always, I say nothing. In keeping my mouth shut, I become an anomaly, an icon. My name is now a code word, not for a run-of-the-mill sex act but for someone who displays an inordinate amount of dignity, someone beautiful and mysterious and slightly dangerous.

After prison I publish a novel under an assumed name. The book is *Lolita* word for word, and I'm allowed to write it because, under the conditions of the fantasy, Vladimir Nabokov never existed. Because it is so magnificent, my book creates a huge stir. Reporters go hunting for the author; when they discover it's me, I think, *Goddamnit, can't you people find any-thing better to do?* I now have a reputation as both a dignified enigma *and* a genius, but I don't want people reading *Lolita* because I wrote it. My masterpiece is demeaned by their pointless search for a hidden autobiographical subtext, so I give up writing, live off of the money I've made from careful stock investments, and quietly spend the rest of my life sleeping with professional football players.

In reviewing these titles, I can't help but notice a few common themes. Looks seem rather important, as does the ability to enlighten, disappoint, and control great numbers of people who always seem to be American. In a city where every woman over the age of fifty has blond hair, my Mr. Science miracle soap would surely have the Parisians lined up all the way to Bethlehem. But it doesn't interest me to manipulate the French. I'm not keyed in to their value system. Because they are not my people, their imagined praise or condemnation means nothing to me. Paris, it seems, is where I've come to dream about America.

My epic fantasies offer the illusion of generosity but never the real thing. I give to some only so I can withhold from others. It's fine to cure the leukemia sufferers but much more satisfying to imagine the parade of opportunists confounded by my refusal to cooperate. In imagining myself as modest, mysterious, and fiercely intelligent, I'm forced to realize that, in real life, I have none of these qualities. Nobody dreams of the things he already has. I'm not sure which is more un-likely: the chance that I'll sleep with the president or the hope that I will one day learn to keep a secret.

There are other fantasies involving magic powers, im-possible wealth, and the ability to sing and dance. Though I can hypnotize the mafia and raise the dead at will, I seem in-capable of erasing the circles beneath my eyes. My dramas don't help me sleep, they simply allow me to pretend that I'm somebody else, someone who's not lying saucer-eyed on a sweat-drenched mattress, watching the minutes flap forward and awaiting the dawn of another dry day.

I'll Eat What He's Wearing

WE'RE IN PARIS, eating dinner in a nice restaurant, and my father is telling a story. "So," he says, "I found this brown something-or-other in my suitcase, and I started chewing on it, thinking that maybe it was part of a cookie."

"Had you packed any cookies?" my friend Maja asks.

My father considers this an irrelevant question and brushes it off, saying, "Not that I know of, but that's not the point."

"So you found this thing in your suitcase, and your first instinct was to put it in your mouth?"

"Well, yes," he says. "Sure I did. But the thing is . . ."

He continues his story but, aside from my sisters and me, his audience is snagged on what would strike any sane adult as a considerable stumbling block. Why would a full-grown man place a foreign object into his mouth, especially if it was brown and discovered in a rarely-used suitcase? It is a reasonable question, partially answered when the coffee arrives and my father slips a fistful of sugar into a pocket of his sport coat. Had my friends seen the blackened banana lying on my bed, they might have understood my father's story and enjoyed it on its own merit. As it stood, however, an explanation was in order.

For as long as I can remember, my father has saved. He saves money, he saves disfigured sticks that resemble disfigured celebrities, and, most of all, he saves food. Cherry tomatoes, sausage biscuits, the olives plucked from other people's martinis — he hides these things in strange places until they are rotten. And then he eats them.

I used to think of this as standard Greek behavior until I realized that ours was the only car in the church parking lot consistently swarmed by bees. My father hid peaches in the trunk. He hid pastries in the toolshed and the laundry room and then wondered where all the ants were coming from. Open the cabinet in the master bathroom, and to this day, you will find expired six-packs of Sego, a chalky dietary milk shake popular in the late sixties. Crowded beside liquefied nectarines and rock-hard kaiser rolls, the cans relax, dented and lint-covered, against the nastiest shaving kit you have ever seen in your life.

There are those who attribute my father's hoarding to

being raised during the Depression, but my mother was not one of them.

"Bullshit," she used to say. "I had it much worse than him, but you don't see *me* hiding figs."

The reference to figs was telling. My father hid them until they assumed the consistency of tar, but why did he bother? No one else in the family would have gone anywhere near a fig, regardless of its age. There were never any potato chips tucked into his food vaults, no chocolate bars or marshmallow figurines. The question, asked continually throughout our childhood, was, Who is he hiding these things from? Aside from the usual insects and the well-publicized starving people in India, we failed to see any potential takers. You wouldn't catch our neighbors scraping mold off their strawberries, but to our father, there was nothing so rotten that it couldn't be eaten. It was people who were spoiled, not food.

"It's fine," he'd say, watching as a swarm of flies deposited their hatchlings into the decaying flesh of a pineapple. "There's nothing wrong with that. I'd eat it!" And he would, if the price was right. And the price was always right.

Because she fell for words like *fresh-picked* and *vine-ripened*, our mother was defined as a spendthrift. You couldn't trust a patsy like that, especially in the marketplace, so, armed with a thick stack of coupons, our father did all the shopping himself. Accompanying him to the grocery store, my sisters and I were encouraged to think of the produce aisle as an all-you-can-eat buffet. Tart apples, cherries, grapes, and unblemished tangerines: he was of the opinion that because they weren't wrapped, these things were free for the taking. The store managers thought differently, and it was always just a matter of time before someone was sent to stop him. The head of the produce department would arrive, and my father, his mouth full of food, would demand to be taken into the back room, a virtual morgue where unwanted food rested between death and burial.

Due to the stench and what our mother referred to as "one small scrap of dignity," my sisters and I rarely entered the back room. It seemed best to distance ourselves, so we would pretend to be other people's children until our father returned bearing defeated fruits and vegetables that bore no resemblance to those he had earlier enjoyed with such abandon. The message was that if something is free, you should take only the best. If, on the other hand, you're forced to pay, it's best to lower the bar and not be so choosy.

"Quit your bellyaching," he'd say, tossing a family pack of anemic pork chops into the cart. "Meat is *supposed* to be gray. They doctor up the color for the ads and so forth, but there's nothing wrong with these. You'll see."

I've never known our father to buy anything not marked REDUCED FOR QUICK SALE. Without that orange tag, an item was virtually invisible to him. The problem was that he never associated "quick sale" with "immediate consumption." Upon returning from the store, he would put the meat into the freezer, hide his favorite fruits in the bathroom cabinet, and stuff everything else into the crisper. It was, of course, too late for crisp, but he took the refrigerator drawer at its word, insisting it was capable of reviving the dead and returning them, hale and vibrant, to the prime of their lives. Subjected to a few days in his beloved crisper, a carrot would become as pale and soft as a flaccid penis.

"Hey," he'd say. "Somebody ought to eat this before it goes bad."

He'd take a bite, and the rest of us would wince at the unnatural silence. Too weak to resist, the carrot quietly surrendered to the force of his jaws. An overcooked hot dog would have made more noise. Wiping the juice from his lips, he would insist that this was the best carrot he'd ever eaten. "You guys don't know what you're missing."

I think we had a pretty good idea.

Even at our most selfish, we could understand why someone might be frugal with six children to support. We hoped our father might ease up and learn to treat himself once we all left home, but, if anything, he's only gotten worse. Nothing will convince him that his fortunes might not suddenly reverse, reducing him to a diet of fingernail clippings or soups made from fallen leaves and seasoned with flashlight batteries. The market will collapse or the crops will fail. Invading armies will go door-to-door, taking even our condiments, yet my father will tough it out. Retired now and living alone, he continues to eat like a scavenging bird.

We used to return home for Christmas every year, my brother, sisters, and I making it a point to call ahead, offering to bring whatever was needed for the traditional holiday meal.

"No, I already got the lamb," our father would say. "Grape leaves, phyllo dough, potatoes — I got everything on the list."

"Yes, but *when* did you get those things?"

An honest man except when it comes to food, our father would lie, claiming to have just returned from the pricey new Fresh Market.

"Did you get the beans?" we'd ask.

"Well, sure I did."

"Let me hear you snap one."

Come Christmas Day, we would fly home to find a leg of lamb thawing beneath six inches of frost, the purchase date revealing that it had been bought midway through the Carter administration. Age had already mashed the potatoes, the grape leaves bore fur, and it was clear that, when spoken to earlier on the phone, our father had snapped his fingers in imitation of a healthy green bean.

"Why the long faces?" he'd ask. "It's Christmas Day. Cheer up, for Christ's sake."

Tired of rancid oleo and "perfectly good" milk resembling blue-cheese dressing, my family began taking turns hosting Christmas dinner. This past year, it was my turn, and those who could afford it agreed to join me in Paris. I met my father's plane at Charles de Gaulle, and as we were walking toward the taxi stand, a bag of peanuts fell from the pouch of his suitcase. These were not peanuts handed out on his recent flight but something acquired years earlier, back when all planes had propellers and pilots wore leather helmets and long, flowing scarves.

I picked up the bag and felt its contents crumble and turn to dust. "Give me those, will you?" My father tucked the peanuts inside his breast pocket, saving them for later.

Back at the apartment, he unpacked. I thought the cat had defecated on my bed until I realized that the object on my pillow was not a turd but a shriveled black banana he had brought all the way to Paris from its hiding place beneath the bathroom sink.

"Here," my father said. "I'll give you half of it."

He'd brought a pear as well and had wrapped it in a plastic bag so that its pus wouldn't stain the clothing he had packed a day earlier but bought long before he was married. As with his food, my father is faithful to his wardrobe. Operating on the assumption that, sooner or later, even the toga will make a comeback, he holds on to his clothing and continues to wear things long after they've begun to disintegrate.

Included in his suitcase was a battered suede cap bought in Kansas City shortly after the war. This was the cap that would figure into his story later that night, when we joined my sisters and a few friends at a nice Paris restaurant.

"So," he says, "I found this brown-colored something-or-other in my suitcase, and I must have chewed on the thing for a good five minutes, until I realized I was eating the brim of my cap. Can you beat that? A piece of it must have broken off during the flight — but hell, how was I supposed to know what it was?"

My friend Maja finds this amusing. "So you literally *ate* your hat?"

"Well, yes," my father says. "But not the whole thing. I stopped after the first few bites."

An outsider might think he stopped for practical reasons, but my sisters and I know better. Because it didn't kill him, the cap had proved edible and would now be savored and appreciated in a different way. No longer considered an article of clothing, it would return to its native land, where it would move from the closet to the bathroom cabinet, joining the ranks of the spoiled to wait for the coming famine.

WHEN YOU ARE ENGULFED IN FLAMES

David Sedaris

David Sedaris's remarkable ability to uncover the hilarious absurdity teeming just below the surface of everyday life is elevated to wilder and more entertaining heights than ever.

Sedaris proceeds from bizarre conundrums of daily life – the etiquette of having a lozenge fall from your mouth into the lap of a fellow passenger or how to soundproof your windows with LP covers against neurotic songbirds – to the most deeply resonant human truths. Taking in the parasitic worm that once lived in his mother-in-law's leg, and culminating in a brilliant account of his attempt to quit smoking – in Tokyo – David Sedaris's sixth story collection is a fresh masterpiece of comic writing.

'A virtual Klondike of darkly glittering anecdotes'
Adam Mars-Jones, *Observer*

ABACUS
978-0-349-11647-1

DRESS YOUR FAMILY IN CORDUROY AND DENIM

David Sedaris

'A humorist par excellence, he can make Woody Allen appear
ham-tongued, Oscar Wilde a drag'
Observer

David Sedaris plays in the snow with his sisters.
He goes on vacation with his family.
He gets a job selling drinks.
He attends his brother's wedding.
He mops his sister's floor.
He gives directions to a lost traveller.
He eats a hamburger.
He has his blood sugar tested.
It all sounds so normal, doesn't it?

In his new book David Sedaris lifts the corner of ordinary
life, revealing the absurdity teeming below its surface. His
world is alive with obscure desires and hidden motives – a
world where forgiveness is automatic and an argument can be
the highest form of love. *Dress Your Family in Corduroy and
Denim* finds one of the wittiest and most original writers at
work today at the peak of his power.

'Very, very funny'
Time Out

'This is one book that cannot fail to hit that elusive spot
which provokes uncontrolled laughter'
The List

ABACUS
978-0-349-11670-9

ABACUS

To buy any of our books and to find out
more about Abacus and Little, Brown, our authors
and titles, as well as events and book clubs,
visit our website

www.littlebrown.co.uk

and follow us on Twitter

@AbacusBooks
@LittleBrownUK

To order any Abacus titles p & p free in the UK,
please contact our mail order supplier on:

+ 44 (0)1832 737525

Customers not based in the UK should contact
the same number for appropriate postage
and packing costs.